If It Moves,
SALUTE IT!

If It Moves, Salute It!

Confessions of a 1950s Royal Navy Conscript

MICHAEL PERRIS

Dedicated to the memory of my wife Anne, who enjoyed a good read.

First published 2011

The History Press
The Mill, Brimscombe Port
Stroud, Gloucestershire, GL5 2QG
www.thehistorypress.co.uk

British Library Cataloguing in Publication Data.
A catalogue record for this book is available from the British Library.

ISBN 978 0 7524 6191 5

Typesetting and origination by The History Press
Printed in the EU for The History Press.

CONTENTS

Acknowledgements

My thanks to Colin and Marina for reading through the draft, pointing out the mistakes for correction, and making invaluable suggestions for improvement. They were even kind enough to encourage me by saying that they enjoyed it. My thanks also to Ian Callow of SETT, Stephen Courtney of the Royal Navy National Museum, and Daniel Lerner of the Gibraltar Tourist Board for their help in providing some of the illustrations.

INTRODUCTION

'Pressed into service means pressed out of shape'
(Robert Frost, 'The Self-Seeker')

I originally wrote most of this book several years ago. In fact, I realise now that it was probably more years ago than I care to remember. I penned it mainly for my own interest and without any ambition to become a writer.

So why did I decide to have it published now, after all this time? Well, there were several reasons, one of which was the fact that the book is about my time as a national serviceman in the late 1950s, and it is coming up to the fiftieth anniversary of the last national serviceman to leave the forces. And there aren't likely to be any more – not for a while anyway, though many people have a sort of nostalgia for the old days and would like to see conscription brought back in again for today's youngsters.

During modern times, there have actually been two separate periods of conscription in the United Kingdom. It was first introduced following the outbreak of the First World War, when the Military Service Act of 1916 decreed that all single men between the ages of eighteen and forty-one were liable for military service – unless they were ministers of a recognised religion or were widowed with dependent children. Before the war was over, the age limit had been raised to fifty-one and married men were no longer exempt. It was not until 1919 that the Act was finally abolished.

And that would have been that if Hitler hadn't decided that he was going to invade Poland some years later. With war seeming inevitable, a number of precautionary steps were decided upon and Parliament passed the Military Training Act in April 1939. This decreed that all single men aged twenty and twenty-one years of age should undergo a six-month period of basic training which would then be augmented by annual refresher courses. Unfortunately, the outbreak of war put a new complexion on this idea and instead Parliament had to pass the National Service Armed Forces Act, which made all men between the ages of eighteen and forty-one liable for conscription. Single men were to be called up before those that were married. Provision was made for those judged to be employed in essential services to be exempted from duty, as well as conscientious objectors. This led to various inconsistencies, as different interpretations were given to the meaning of 'essential services' and to various objections to serving with the military. At one stage, conscripts known as 'Bevin Boys' (named after the wartime Labour Minister Ernest Bevin) were even drafted into the coal mining industry. Nevertheless, by the end of 1939 over 1.5 million recruits had been drafted into the forces, over a million of whom had gone into the army. By 1942 call-up had been extended to men aged eighteen to fifty-one and women from twenty to thirty years old. In theory this included pregnant women, but there weren't any examples in practice.

By the end of 1945, when the war was at long last over, all women were released from duty, together with skilled men who were needed urgently for trades such as building etc. Some form of conscription carried on and it wasn't until 1949 that the last wartime conscript was finally released back into civilian life. But that was not to be the end of conscription. The National Service Act was inaugurated in 1948 and it required all fit and healthy males from the ages of seventeen to twenty-one to serve in the armed forces for a period of eighteen months. They were then to remain on a list of reserves to be called up in the event of a conflict. By late 1950, largely as a result of the Korean War, the period of training and service had been increased to two years and national servicemen served with distinction in a number of combats around the world, including spells in Cyprus, Kenya, Malaya and the Battle of the Imjin River, as well as in Korea. Officially conscription finally ended in December 1960, but due to deferrals, the crisis at the time of the erection of the Berlin Wall and a general confusion over periods already served, the last conscript left the Army Pay Corps on 13 May 1963. The honour of that place in history went to a Lieutenant Richard Vaughan.

At this time, the view of the regular armed forces about conscription was clear enough, though I don't suppose it had anything to do with my service. You could almost hear the sigh of relief coming from the direction of Admiralty House when, a short time after I was 'demobbed', it was announced that they were going to end all national service. Then, to the Civil Service's dismay, it was discovered that there were still a number of excused draftees left over that they had overlooked.

Some youngsters' service had previously been deferred for a year or two because of various health, college, family or job-related problems and so it was not until May 1963 that the last national serviceman quit the services – from the army. The navy had long since stopped taking any more conscripts, citing as a reason that the short period was insufficient for the thorough training of recruits in that branch of the military.

But this book is not just about national service. It's also about a way of life and a lot of traditions which are fast disappearing from the modern navy. It seemed a pity not to record some of them before they vanish for ever and the many priceless episodes which interspersed a somewhat routine life at sea bear testimony to the fact that it wasn't all work. I've tried to give my story a flavour of what it was like to wear bell-bottoms, go for a 'run ashore' and afterwards to try and climb up into a hammock. How it felt to curse your mates when they are the pretend enemy in a war game, and were dropping grenades on to the casing of your submarine to let you know that you've been detected and destroyed. It's then that you realise that next time it could be for real! Throughout, I've tried to tell it as it was; warts and all, some may think!

I should confess that I wasn't personally involved in every escapade described herein. Some of the events were recounted to me by fellow servicemen and so I can't vouch that it wasn't coloured a bit in the telling. I have used fictitious names for many of the characters I met and shared time with. It seemed kinder and fairer that way!

Oh, and the final reason for only now bringing out a book written about events that happened fifty years ago, was that the publishers also thought it made a good story. I hope you do too!

★★★

The opinions expressed by characters in this book are neither those of the author nor the publisher and are included to illustrate the period described. Occasionally, language used is 'of its time' and is not intended to cause offence.

Chapter 1

Your Country Needs You

A plaque on the desk claimed that the man sitting behind it and regarding me rather quizzically was a Chief Petty Officer Davies. I wasn't sure about the importance of a petty officer in the navy's hierarchy, let alone a chief, but I guessed that it probably wouldn't be a good idea to get it wrong. He certainly looked very smart in a double-breasted, dark navy blue suit, with gold-coloured buttons and complementary gold lapel badges. His white-topped, peaked cap, complete with more gold badges, had been placed on the desk in front of him. I thought: 'I could look good in a uniform like that.'

I hesitated for a moment, not knowing quite how much respect to show.

'Can I help you sir?' he enquired, saving me the trouble. I probably didn't realise it at the time, but it was going to be quite a while before anyone called me 'sir' again.

I showed him the official-looking letter of introduction that I had received.

'I suppose you want the army or the air force,' he said, rather caustically I thought. But he seemed to perk up a bit when I told him that I had thought more in terms of the navy.

It didn't seem a good idea to tell him I believed the navy might be the least worst choice of the three. I had sat through all those heroic navy films with John Mills and Richard Attenborough, and although it looked as though it might not be all that safe at sea, it was probably better than either of the alternatives. Anyway, I'd heard you got cheap cigarettes in the navy!

'I've been thinking about joining the navy for some time,' I said eventually, trying to look a bit like John Mills. I even half-believed it myself. I had heard somewhere that it was the most difficult of the services to get into, so logically it should be the best choice. At least I would probably be some way away from home. Not that I was particularly desperate to get away, but I rather liked the idea of free travel.

'Isn't it called the senior service?' I asked hastily – and probably a bit inanely. At the time it was all I could think of to say. I had been looking at the recruitment slogans on the way in – and illogically remembered the brand of cigarettes with the same name.

'Have any of your relatives served in the navy?' he asked. He didn't sound very concerned either way.

'Yes I think so,' I said, remembering that an uncle of mine had once served in the Royal Navy during the war – or maybe it was the Merchant Navy, I couldn't be sure. Luckily he didn't seem greatly interested anyway.

'You'll have to have a medical,' he said doubtfully. 'We've got a doctor here at the moment, so if you go and wait in reception we'll do it now.'

I joined three or four others who were sitting on chairs in a row near the door. From here they were called one at a time into a side room, but it was nearly an hour later before my name was called and the receptionist said I should go in and see the doctor.

I stripped to the waist as directed and presented my body for inspection. The short, elderly doctor regarded it quizzically through thick, rimless glasses and then, not content with merely looking, he proceeded to first prod it and then press the end of a stethoscope against various parts of my front and back. After some more thumping with his fingertips on the back of a hand placed at various strategic parts of my body, he pronounced himself satisfied and we moved on to the next stage.

As instructed, I sat down on a chair opposite him and alternately crossed one leg over the other while he tapped on the knee with a rubber hammer and watched to see what reaction it provoked. I gathered from his expression that everything so far was in good working order. Then I stood up again as directed and dropped my trousers and underpants to the floor. It was then that I began to get concerned. The doctor held my privates in one hand and told me to turn my head alternatively to each side and cough. At the time I assumed that this was all part of a vital medical test, but later I wasn't so sure. It even crossed my mind that perhaps he just liked doing it. I hastily pulled my trousers back up and hoped he'd washed his hands!

'How do I stand, Doc?' I asked, trying to sound unconcerned.

With pursed lips, he seemed lost in thought. 'That's just what has been puzzling me too,' he finally remarked. As he burst out laughing, I realised it was his little medical joke.

Before I could think of a suitable reply he led me next door to a dimly lit room where he announced that he was going to check my hearing. I stood in one corner while he first whispered something in the opposite corner and then asked if I had heard what he had said. I told him that it had sounded to me as if he was reciting the days of the week, which appeared to be the right answer. He declared that I had passed the hearing test.

There didn't seem much else of me to check, except of course my eyes, and eventually they got round to those as well. First of all I had a test for colour-blindness. At the time, the significance of whether I could distinguish between red and green escaped me, but months later I was to find out. In any case I satisfied them on that point and moved on to the eye chart. By now, I was beginning to enjoy myself and had hardly got past reading off the first two or three rows of letters before I was declared fit in all departments. I wasn't sure whether to be glad or sorry, but as it turned out it didn't seem to matter either way, and a month later I got a letter telling me to report for duty to HMS *Raleigh*. As an afterthought the note suggested I should bring along my own toothbrush and shaving gear...

I was nineteen years old and had just failed the first year's exams at college. At that age you rarely know for certain what you want to do in life. You're too old and grown up for being a 'teen', but somehow you're not yet ready to conform to being an adult. So until I had made up my mind, I had decided to take a job driving a delivery van for an electrical wholesalers in Brighton.

One winter's evening, probably driving too fast along dark Sussex lanes in the rain, I had gone around a corner and suddenly came across a cow standing in the middle of the road. It must have strayed out of its field, or something, but it was an even bet as to which of us was the more confused. I swerved to try and avoid the obstacle and at that moment the cow decided to panic – closely followed by me. As it tried to get past there was a crash against the side of the van and, with me still hanging on to the steering wheel for dear life, we all ended up on the grass verge.

Apart from the cow's dignity and my pride, nothing else appeared to have been hurt. The only damage was to the side of the van. So, after a few moments I drove on and hoped it wouldn't come to anything. The cow meanwhile had given me a disdainful look and ambled off into the night. To make things worse, I didn't get much sympathy when I turned up at work the next day either. They even suggested that I should get some glasses.

A week later I got a message to go to the manager's office.

'It's your lucky day,' said Mr Daniels as I entered. 'This time…' he added, slowly and rather ominously, I thought. 'The insurance will pay for the damage, and the company has decided not to take it any further.'

It had been a couple of weeks ago now and there was still a bit of a dent in the side of the van. As the evening papers had put it succinctly, 'the vehicle had come into contact with a farm animal'.

Inwardly I breathed a sigh of relief. Happily for me, it looked as if the company couldn't believe that a cow had caused the damage, but failing any other cause they had decided to give me the benefit of the doubt. Things seemed to be looking up, after all.

I found that my optimism was short-lived. The very next day I got a letter in the post saying that as I was over the age of eighteen and as I was no longer in full-time education, I might be liable for national service instead. I had been half-expecting this to happen, but it was still a bit of a shock when the official letter actually landed on the doormat. I was instructed to go along in a week's time for an interview at the nearest employment office. If necessary they would probably arrange to give me a medical check-up as well. Presumably to see if I was fit enough to die for my country, I thought; but at least they were very polite about it.

I had the distinct feeling that I'd only just got over one problem and blow me if I hadn't landed in the thick of it again! It looked as if I was to be a victim of 'Murphy's second law' which, if I remember correctly, states that for every cloud with a silver lining there's often another one waiting around the corner when you've gone out without a raincoat.

Over the next few days I had to endure the mock salutes and military jokes of my fellow workers. So it was with some trepidation that I got a day off work and caught the bus to the local labour and employment office, which apparently doubled up as a forces recruitment centre. Here my fate was to be decided and by the time I had caught the bus back home again, the die had been cast. It seemed that I would be spending the next two years in the navy. I just hoped that it wouldn't be anything like the film *Two Years Before the Mast*.

CHAPTER 2

IF IT DOESN'T MOVE – WHITEWASH IT

According to the address and instructions that I had received in the post, HMS *Raleigh* was located somewhere near Plymouth on the Devon coast. And so, following a fairly long and tedious journey by train and ferry, I eventually stepped down from the local bus and out into pouring rain at the gates of what I now discovered was a naval camp and not a ship at all. Apart from a lack of barbed wire, it reminded me of the PoW camps that were shown in the popular war films of the time.

Lines of dark wooden huts disappeared into the misty distance. On the right-hand side, just inside the wooden entrance gates, stood a larger hut which I later learned was the guard house. Next to it there appeared to be a reception and an administration block where I reported. Then, after completing and signing various forms (which appeared to make the Admiralty responsible for any disasters that might befall me while in their care), I was directed towards yet more huts known as the New Entry Block. This, it transpired, was to be my home for the next six months while I completed initial training. By the end of that period, I had learnt how to march in a straight line, how to wash my under-pants, to interpret orders, fall in line, get up, go to bed, repair my own socks, iron concertina-looking trouser creases, cope with bullies, sleep in a hammock instead of a bed, avoid getting the pox and any number of other things that they said would come in handy in later life.

For the next two years, in fact, they would become an integral part of my life in the forces. Some of the things I spent time practising, seemed at the time to be pretty silly and unnecessary but later, I learnt that they perhaps had more relevance than I had realised. Throughout the rest of that first day a lot more, rather dejected-looking initiates like me, arrived spasmodically at the camp. Some came late, some got lost on the way, and two didn't turn up at all!

As more new recruits arrived we tentatively started to chat and get to know each other. It soon became clear that we were a pretty motley crowd, certainly not suited to any sort of disciplined combat. There was Tim Reynolds, who had been to a minor public school somewhere, hated it and wanted instead to be a farmer. The last thing he wanted was to waste his time doing national service. Then there was Phil Roberts the Teddy boy, with long sideburns, Brylcreemed and combed-back hair, strangulated clothes and 'winklepicker' shoes. He didn't mind being there – for a time anyway, while they stopped looking for him! He stole anything that belonged to authority, but wouldn't think of stealing from his 'mates'. There were apprentices, milkmen and assistant lorry drivers. There were a couple of young unemployed mine workers and a trainee bank clerk. In fact anyone who couldn't skive out of doing his time in the forces or managed to fail the medical examination for one reason or another. There were even a few youngsters who were looking forward to it! By the end of the evening, we had all shared each other's problems, said goodbye to civvy street and most had resigned themselves to what we all agreed would be two wasted years.

Next morning, once we'd breakfasted and collected our clothing issue, we changed and assembled on the parade ground. We had gathered that we were there to learn all about marching and drill. Sheepishly we gathered in front of a chief petty officer and formed ourselves into three shambling, more-or-less straight lines. Meanwhile, the chief just stood there silently, his hands behind his back, and his head thrust forward in a slightly menacing attitude. The neck beneath his well pulled-down cap was sweating and swathed in a dirty bandage.

At last he came to life, gave a sort of twisted grin and bellowed out: 'My name's Burt. Some people call me Burt the bastard. Soon you'll be finding out why.'

He gave us another lengthy examination, slowly walking up and down along the irregular lines of new recruits.

'Gawd,' he exclaimed loudly at last. 'I've seen better formations in the *Come Dancing* programme on telly. You look like an advert for birth control.'

He scowled at Shepherd. 'Unless you are about to change sex,' he called out, 'clasp your hands behind your back when you stand at ease, not in front of you. Only Wrens stand like that, and they have a very good reason.' I discovered that Wrens were members of the Women's Royal Navy and during the course of the next couple of years I not only had to learn new words, but a whole new language.

CPO Burt paused for a moment while he gathered his thoughts. Then, after giving us the benefit of another scowl, he began what I soon realised was his standard welcome to all new recruits.

'Now, let me make this clear,' he shouted, 'I'm going to make your lives bloody miserable. If you've any ideas about enjoying yourselves on the parade ground – forget them. You're here to work and I'll see that you do. You've got two weeks to learn what the regulars learn in five, but you're going to do it better than them. You're going to do it until you get it right, see. I haven't had a failure yet and I promise you I'll not get one this time either.'

It was the longest speech I was to hear him make during the next two weeks – without a stream of abuse and swearing, that is!

'You play ball with me and I'll play ball with you,' I heard 'Taffy' Edwards whisper behind me. A little too loudly, as it turned out. I grinned; and that was to be my first mistake.

The chief marched straight up to me and, with his now-reddening face only inches from mine, bellowed out, 'So you think it's funny do you?'

'No Chief,' I managed to answer, reasoning that it wasn't a good idea to have a clash with authority on your first day.

'Well,' he shouted, 'see if you find running round the parade ground twice, funny instead. AT THE DOUBLE!' he bellowed. There seemed no alternative but to obey his orders. I started off at a jog around the vast tarmac square.

By the time I was about halfway around I began to realise that I had learned two important lessons – lessons which would largely influence my next couple of years. First of all, I began to realise that the career servicemen, who were in charge, didn't have much time for us 'temporaries'. During our training, we were mostly under the watchful eyes of either petty officers or chief petty officers, who weren't really commissioned officers in the traditional sense. Perhaps as a result, they mostly considered us a bit of a distraction from normal service life and a waste of their time and efforts. From their point of view, we wouldn't be there long enough to be of any real use!

The next thing I become conscious of was that if I tried to play the fool with the POs and CPOs in charge, I was going to have a miserable time for the next two years. There and then I resolved to keep my head down and bend with the wind of authority instead of railing against it. As I often heard said later, 'You can't beat the system'.

I completed my two laps of the parade ground and rejoined the others without another word.

At the time of my original arrival at the camp and during my initial appraisal, I had happened to mention that I'd studied a bit of engineering. At that point they decided that I should join the mechanical engineering branch, known to everyone else in the navy as 'stokers' – though there wasn't much to stoke these days. I'd actually said that I had done a bit of electrical engineering, but they presumably had enough people already in the electrical branch. Or perhaps it was just the navy's sense of humour.

Throughout the next few weeks I kept my head down and managed to keep out of any further trouble. There were weeks of intensive activity, with a series of tuition and lectures in naval practice both in the class-room and outside. I became recruit number P/K955741 and I collected the rest of my kit. I was taught to keep my bed and locker tidy, my boots polished and my uniform ironed. I did my 'square-bashing', darned my socks with the 'housewife' kit of needle and thread with which I had been issued and learned to talk in the vernacular. I discovered that ordinary sailors were in fact 'matelots' and that petty officers were POs. On the other hand, they could be 'chiefs' if they were chief petty officers and even 'pussers' if they were in charge of provisions or stores.

In naval parlance, turning to the left was in fact 'going to port', toilets were 'heads', watertight doors in ships were 'hatches' and going out into the wide world outside our camp (or ship) was 'going ashore'. The time of day was divided into a number of periods, marked by the sounding of bells over the loudspeaker or 'tannoy' system. The 'first dogwatch' at sea was the period between 4 and 6a.m in the morning and the 'second dogwatch' between the hours of 6 and 8p.m. Then there were the middle, morning, forenoon and afternoon bells or watches. Even more strangely, dog watches only lasted two hours and were split into a series of differently numbered, half-hourly 'bells', whilst other watches lasted up to four hours. Windows were 'portholes', whilst the lowest form of an officer was a 'Tiffy' or Artificer. The officer in charge of a ship was referred to as 'Jimmy', or the skipper, but rather confusingly, he didn't necessarily have the rank of a captain at all.

Early on, I was shown how to use a pay-book to measure the width of the concertina-type creases in my bell-bottom trousers – although by the late 1970s they had been replaced by 'flares'. In preparation for the restricted spaces on board a ship, I learned how to string a hammock. Eventually, we would have to use them instead of beds but luckily it turned out that they were really quite comfortable if they had been pre-pared properly.

An essential part of my basic training seemed to involve learning to swear regularly, preferably the navy way. Not just ordinary swearing – I knew how to do that before I joined up – but real, imaginative swear-ing. I discovered some new and interesting names for parts of the male and female anatomy and eventually got the hang of turning every third or fourth word into a profanity. I even managed the knack of inserting a swear word between everyday terms, such as petty friggin' officer, but failed miserably when it came to inserting swear words in the middle of other words. Two of the less offensive examples I encountered in the first few weeks were the 'kitsoddingbags' that we had been issued with and the 'lieubloodytenant' who was in charge of our group.

During my early induction as a stoker, I discovered that the cardinal sin as far as my branch of the service was concerned, was to be involved in a ship 'making smoke'. It was pretty much equivalent to having a car with a smoky exhaust, but in the navy it was considered to be a far worse transgression. It was a sign of inefficient burning of fuel and would make a ship more visible to an enemy. It was explained to us graphically by the chief instructor: 'You can do what you like in the boiler room except make smoke. You can open the air lock and let all the air rush out 'til the boiler blows back in yer face. But you mustn't make smoke. The boiler room can even be six inches deep in fuel oil, and you go an' drop yer bloody fag in it. But remember, if any smoke comes out of the funnel when you are at sea you'll be up to your arm-pits in gold braid before the smoke's cleared the top of the stack. The only time it's all right to make smoke, see, 'cos you can't avoid it, is when you are striking up the boiler. And then you get every bloody colour. I mind the time I was striking up while we was out in Gib', and the lieutenant comes blazing into the boiler room. It was his first trip, see, and he was as green as they make 'em. He'd been a bloody bank manager or something in civvy street. I think he'd only been sailing weekends before he joined up. Anyway, "You're making smoke," he yells at me. "Black and white smoke," he says. "You wait here a few minutes," I says, "and I'll make you friggin' yellow smoke as well." Mind you, I wasn't bein' disrespectful, see – I did call 'im Sir.'

As it happened, I didn't have to worry too much about this particular problem since I hardly ever saw a boiler room throughout my naval career.

Before a week had passed in New Entry Block, we were instructed to load up all our gear into kit bags and, together with another 60lb of bedding, we carried them over to our new home in Valiant Block. An alternative name coined for it by Taffy Edwards was Stalag Luft 2½ and it was right over on the other side of the camp. Like it or not, it was here in Room 23 that I was to spend the rest of my time at HMS *Raleigh*. I remained there until I had completed the rest of my basic training and ultimately my first real taste of navy life.

CHAPTER 3

SUITABLE OFFICER MATERIAL

Meanwhile, our training carried on as before. For the next few weeks, each day was much the same as the previous one, with a series of lectures, practical instruction in the workshops, further intensive drill practice on the parade ground, gymnastics and the occasional periods for laundering clothes, ironing and writing letters home. During all that time, we were confined to our increasingly claustrophobic barracks at HMS *Raleigh*.

After a while, I began to get used to the rather strange life and unpredictable ways of the navy. Even so, I was still a bit surprised to discover one day that a few of us had mysteriously been picked to go on what the instructors called 'an intensive initiative training and testing course'. The mood changed when we found out that it was going to be held outside our camp, and by the time it came to pack up our kit we were looking forward to the break. The camp transport took us to the station at Plymouth and after we had been issued with tickets, we caught the train to Portsmouth, bound for the Victoria barracks in Southsea.

The drawn blinds on our compartment soon drew the attention of a passing ticket inspector, but the offer of a drink soon persuaded him to join us in a game of poker. The journey passed quickly and by the time we reached our destination he had little left but his ticket punch and an alcoholic smile. Judging by his happy expression and parting wave, he still seemed to think that it had been worth it.

Victoria barracks looked out over the sea towards the Isle of Wight. It had been built in the previous century by a party of convicts from the local gaol – to which it bore a remarkable resemblance, according to its occupants. On the western side, for an added touch of character, were the nearby twin stacks of the local power station.

Our mess measured roughly 30ft by 30ft. Into this area were crammed eight double-tiered bunks, sixteen lockers, a variety of odd shelves, an ancient wireless and, in the middle of the room for heating during the winter, a large, round stove. Its chimney was bent at right-angles before it disappeared through a hole in the outside wall. Next door, in a bare, draughty room, stood a single ancient lavatory, while along one wall of the nearby bathroom stood a total of eight chipped washbasins. They were to cater for the sixty-odd people crammed into the block's complement of three downstairs messes. The messes on the floor above us were occupied by POs who, I was glad to see, had their own ablutions.

Since we were supposed to be navy stokers on an initiative course, we were naturally expected to try and get the recalcitrant stove alight by ourselves. In the end it took a mixture of white spirit and a large tin of pusser's floor polish to finally get it glowing red-hot, with flames roaring up the chimney and outside into the night air.

We discovered later that the barracks had initially been occupied by the army and had been badly damaged by enemy bombs during the Second World War. As a result they had at one stage been condemned for demolition. To add to its colourful history, the barracks were later taken over by the navy, who didn't really have any plans for it and in any case weren't prepared to spend any money on refurbishing the buildings. Ironically, some time after we had occupied the facilities, it was again condemned and finally given back to the army.

Not being aware of any of this colourful background at the time, we did our best to settle into the temporary home. We found that nearby, in another part of the barracks, lived a contingent of wrens. Unlike the national servicemen or the full-time servicemen, they didn't have to sign up for any kind of permanent, long-term contract. Consequently, they could hand in their uniforms and leave the service at a moment's notice if they felt so inclined.

So to try and make sure they didn't do anything of the sort, the navy naturally afforded them with every incentive to stay. They were provided with all manner of luxuries that we could only dream about, such as comfortably fitted-out lounges, reading rooms, bedrooms with proper wardrobes and their own individual chest of drawers. The wrens even had baths and modern toilet facilities. The coal fires were lit for them and were regularly restocked by sailors who were detailed for the task. All the while the incumbents' virginity was protected at night time by duty guards patrolling the whole area. Much to the annoyance of the wrens, of course, who at the time were busy trying to lose it!

During the warmer summer months, they often forgot to close the curtains in their bedrooms. For some reason, they also seemed to have a habit of wearing very little clothing. Consequently, the patrolling sentries had to be instructed to keep everyone, including themselves, well away from any lighted windows. It was a task they managed to perform with very little success! It wasn't long before we realised that the wrens' eyes were set firmly on the resident officers and their charms were not to be wasted on ordinary ranks. Even the most ardent of our group failed to get any further than the door to their quarters, where they were faced by a notice warning everyone to 'abandon hope all ye who enter here'. Wrens, it appeared, were off-limits! By the time that we had settled into the new quarters, we discovered that it didn't really matter anyway, since we hadn't been sent there to admire the wrens. The 'initiative tests' were, in fact an officer selection trial. It appeared that we had been sent there to see if any of us could become suitable officer material. It didn't take very long to find out.

Over the next three days we were set a variety of tests. They ranged from a general knowledge assessment, to a mathematics ability check, an initiative test and a personal presentation. Finally there was to be an interview with a panel of high-ranking officers and a psychologist. It was worse than having a tooth pulled!

I started off all right with the written test and even though the relevance didn't seem obvious, I managed to answer most of the general knowledge questions. These included queries about where the Queen Mother stayed in London, who painted the *Mona Lisa* and which flowers could be affected by rust or disease.

Afterwards there were a series of maths tests which seemed to be a bit more useful if you were going to be a naval officer. Thankfully they were fairly basic calculations, since it seemed that officers didn't need to do many sums. After lunch, we sat what they called a PSO test. This involved completing a number of optional statements such as: 'Hot is to cold as bad is to – choose either a) worthless b) good c) indifferent or d) spaghetti.' These, and other questions like them, took up the rest of the first day and by the end I felt rather smug with myself. I seemed to have completed most of the papers – at least to my satisfaction. Unfortunately, any feeling of elation was to be short-lived.

Next morning, we moved on to HMS *Ciscern* in nearby Gosport. It was there that they had arranged for the initiative tests, together with a group discussion on four different subjects, lasting five minutes at a time. We were told that on the third and final day, as well as facing an interview, we would have to prepare a five-minute talk on a subject of the board's choosing. We would get no more than three minutes to prepare for the presentation beforehand. In the end I flopped lamentably in all of them.

It appeared that the secret to being a good officer often involved getting a large oil drum and a team of men from one platform across a pretend swamp to another about 30ft away. In order to accomplish this feat, I was given a pile of planks and a few ropes and I had a team of six under my command. Also, since the test took place in the camp gymnasium, the 'swamp' inexplicably included a set of parallel bars in the middle. The aim was to get drum and team, including myself, to the other side of the swamp in under ten minutes. Since it felt more like competing in a television game show, rather than a chance to display my powers of initiative and reason, I probably didn't take it as seriously as I should have done. I did manage to get two of the team drowned in the swamp in well under the allotted time, but it didn't seem to count in my favour. Also I only got the rest of us across, together with the oil drum, when one of the group who had done the exercise before at the Dartmouth training school, whispered in my ear. The other teams didn't seem to do much better, but the damage was done.

I didn't have any more success when it came to giving a five-minute talk on 'autumn', the subject which I had been allocated. It took me about half a minute to cover most of what I could think of to say on the subject and another painfully long two and a half minutes of repetitions or 'Um's' and 'Ah's'. In the afternoon we had a discussion session, with a number of bored listeners in the background. Of the topics that were raised, only 'Today's Teddy boys' seemed to produce any real sort of lively discussion. It soon became apparent that some of the others had a far more intimate knowledge of the subject than I did, apart from what I had read in the papers. As a consequence, I wasn't able to contribute much. The day hadn't gone very well and it didn't get any better the next day either.

When it came to my turn to face the interview board, I realised early on that I was failing to impress the high-powered panel of interviewers. The board consisted of three lieutenant commanders, a captain and the psychologist who sat at the back of the room and picked his nails. Apart from my lack of family connections with the navy and distinct lack of any higher education, it appeared that my reluctance to commit to a long-term commission in the service didn't help either. Once I had confirmed this fact any hope of officer status quickly evaporated and by the time it was all over the only crumb of consolation was that no one else on the course did any better either.

I packed my bags once more and went back to HMS *Raleigh* to continue my basic training where I had left off. Some of it was held on the naval property known as Whale Island, where we went for a course on fire-fighting and to learn about the different types of dangerous 'war' gases to which we could be exposed. It all came under the heading of Atomic, Biological, Chemical Defence and Damage Control.

'First, we're going to show you some lovely films,' said the chief instructor. If we had expected the latest Hollywood epic, we were to be very disappointed.

We sat and watched gory films about the accidents that could occur on board ships. A lot of them seemed to involve severed fingers or other limbs. Apparently they could result from falling, unsecured hatch covers, blowbacks from boilers or falling into unprotected machinery. Then there were other films about the nasty effects of sexually transmitted diseases (including close-ups of rotting private parts). If they were intended to put us off joining the navy permanently, they certainly succeeded!

Afterwards, to cheer us up a bit, they told us all about the various nerve, blister and choking gases etc. we might meet. It included, of course, the different fatal effects they would have on us. We were told when to use our respirator, when to apply the special ointment atropin and (most usefully) that with gases such as CTC and carbon monoxide, the respirator would be of no help whatsoever. Encouragingly, the chief also confided in us that the most efficient nerve gases were both colourless and odourless. If we were ever exposed to them, he informed us happily, we would only have a few seconds to apply any safety measures before they took affect anyway – which, of course, would be terminal!

We gathered that we would stand a bit more chance with the so-called 'nose' gases and choking gases such as chlorine and DM or DC as they were called. They at least could be spotted by their pretty colours and sometimes by their smell as well.

By this time, the instructor had really warmed to his subject. 'The nose gasses aren't nearly as bad,' he told us, 'they'll only cause choking or perhaps give you a headache. Of course,' he added, 'they'll probably irritate your eyes and maybe make you partially blind for a while, but they won't kill you.'

He seemed to think that this was good news and it came as something of a relief to his audience. Then he rather spoilt it all by telling us that any encounter with blister gases would be far worse. Lewisite, he assured us, or 'L' gas as it was sometimes known, was 'really nasty stuff'. He then got on to the effects of exposure to radiation, which apparently involved sickness, seeping open sores, blindness and lingering death. By that time I was beginning to wonder whether I had chosen the safest of career moves.

Happily the next day's fire-fighting, by comparison, was almost a light-hearted affair, with lots of smoke and flames shooting up into the sky from great big metal pans of burning oil. There were fire-fighting-suited figures, masses of hoses, fire extinguishers and spraying water everywhere. Not only did we learn all about the differences between chemical, electrical and oil-based fires, but we also got to spray foam or water all over each other as well as on the fires. We put on breathing apparatus and gas masks, ran through burning buildings and were then exposed to some of the less-lethal gases to sample their effects first-hand. We seized on the opportunity to create every sort of mayhem and pyrotechnics for the best part of three days. For many of the group it was the first opportunity they had had for several months to get out of our barracks and 'let off steam' – and it was all with the Admiralty's blessing. This was a chance not to be missed and we were almost sorry when it was over. For a while we had forgotten why we were there and it had felt like being let loose in a chocolate factory!

CHAPTER 4

A Break in Security

Back at *Raleigh* we carried on with the round of lectures, kit inspections, parade drill, a variety of sports and any other activities that the navy could think of to keep us occupied. Then, as if to break the monotony, we learned one morning that an exercise had been devised to test out the security of the camp. The camp had enlisted the help of the local marine commandos who had agreed to attempt a raid on us.

To add a bit more interest and also make it more realistic, the only detail the organisers disclosed was that it would be scheduled to start sometime after midday on the following day. At the time, it all sounded innocuous enough. We would just have to be a bit extra vigilant and keep an eye open for any strangers around the camp. No sweat, as the instructor said!

The very next morning as the time agreed for the raid approached, extra guards were posted around the perimeter fence. The camp gates were closed and anyone entering the barracks was carefully checked. Patrols of sailors were sent out to scour the approaches to the camp and the nearby countryside. All those taking part were issued with field packs and unloaded rifles. We were prepared for anything – or so we thought! The lanes and hedgerows surrounding the camp were bristling with uniformed sailors. Innocent citizens going about their business were pounced upon from all sides under suspicion of being commandos in disguise. Nothing was left to chance.

Unfortunately, unbeknown to us, on a building site next to the perimeter fence and a couple of hundred yards away from the camp's entrance, some of the commandos, dressed up as workmen, were making their own preparations. Another group of 'workmen' were busily digging a ditch not far from the gates themselves. By mid-afternoon there were more marine commandos inside the camp than there were sailors. They had come in on bicycles pretending to be postmen or civilian workmen, and had gone undetected at the gates. At the same time the disguised marines, who were out of sight on the building site alongside the perimeter fence, had used the site's mobile crane to swing them up in a large skip and over the fence.

Other commandos had captured sailors outside the camp and borrowed their uniforms to help them get inside. They even persuaded the guard at the gates to put down his rifle whilst he helpfully gave one of the 'workmen' a hand with moving the ceremonial cannon, all the while conveniently out of sight of the guardhouse. Much to his embarrassment, he too ended up as a captive, unceremoniously bundled into the marines' truck and replaced with one of their own group, equipped now with the guard's own rifle. Both he and the rifle were duly returned once the exercise was over, but the damage had been done by then.

We found out later that more infiltrators had come into the camp the night before the exercise was officially meant to start. Disguised as some of the soldiers who had fought alongside the navy in the Middle East during the Second World War, they had been welcomed in and treated to drinks by some of the POs who had actually been there. After a few drinks, some of the petty officers even thought they remembered the 'soldiers' as old comrades.

After a night spent celebrating and reminiscing, the POs left them to find their own way out of the camp while they went to bed. Of course, what they didn't know was that the commandos had spent the rest of the night lying under the same unsuspecting petty officers' huts. In the morning they changed again and became civilian workmen, going about their ordinary business inside the camp and passing useful details about the navy's security measures on the phone to their colleagues outside. A diversionary fire was started with some drums of waste oil and cardboard boxes that they had found behind one of the huts, which provided an impressive display of flames and smoke. The camp's own fire brigade were at the time being augmented by the town's fire crew and they were duly summoned by the duty officer. Naturally more commandos were then able to get inside the camp, disguised as firemen.

The last straw probably came when the commandos managed to capture the camp's mascot, a long-haired white goat. They proceeded to get the animal thoroughly drunk, by the simple expedient of adding large quantities of beer to its bowl of milk. That evening, after the goat had been returned to its rightful owners, it staggered into the officers' dining room and was promptly sick all over the carpet. It then lay down and went to sleep. The final indignity was that while the mascot was in captivity, the raiders had managed to feed it on a plentiful supply of garlic, so that the goat's breathe smelled for days afterwards.

No one was really surprised when it was decided not to hold any more security exercises whilst we were at HMS *Raleigh*. The hastily revised security arrangements were still being put into effect a week later when, to round off our basic training, we were given a taste of shipboard living. It would mean spending a week or so on board HMS *Sluys*, a battle-class destroyer. The *Sluys* had been commissioned as long ago as 1946 and now, after a pretty varied career, was anchored nearby in Plymouth estuary. It had been named after a battle fought against the French during the Hundred Years War but I'm not sure we would have appreciated the honour even if we had known about its background.

On board HMS *Sluys* we discovered what it was like to live, eat and sleep together in possibly the most cramped conditions devised since convicts had been transported to the colonies. Until then, I hadn't thought it possible to pack so much inside a steel-lined space, measuring some 40ft long by about 20ft wide and perhaps 9 or 10ft high. As well as our living quarters there was also a fire main pump in one corner, running day and night, several miles of pipe-work, cables and tubes which criss-crossed the walls and roof. The 'mess', as it was called, also held an air-conditioning plant, hundreds of junction boxes and valves, four tables, some chairs and benches, thirty lockers, numerous shelves and cupboards, a wireless, lockers full of plates, cups, cutlery and food, and a tannoy system.

That still had to leave room for thirty people together with their hammocks, bedding, kit cases and personal effects. Some previous occupants had left their mark behind and from every spare bit of space on the bulkhead walls, pictures of smiling, large-bosomed, heavy-hipped girls looked down on us. We were able to admire plunging necklines from America, icy blondes in bathing costumes from Sweden, girls playing with beach balls, Coca-Cola girls and girls sunbathing on far-off Pacific sands having apparently forgotten to pack their swimsuits.

Outside, as far as the eye could see along the estuary where the *Sluys* was anchored, there were long lines of silent, battle-grey ships.

They strained against the tides at the end of their anchor chains, while inside their hulls were billions of pounds worth of military equipment. Battleships, cruisers, aircraft carriers, frigates and destroyers – all silently waiting for a call to sail. Some of the names of the more famous ships like the *Melbourne*, the *Howe* and the *Ark Royal* already had their entries in naval history and even I had heard of them.

We spent the next week or two getting used to shipboard living and at the same time practising boiler room procedures and the starting up and running of the enormous range of auxiliary equipment that a ship seemed to carry. As stokers, we were responsible for the pumps, generators, refrigerating equipment and all the other mechanical devices on board as well as the boilers and turbines which we had already covered in basic training.

It was well into December by now and the weather was getting colder. Soon it would be Christmastime and everyone was beginning to think about getting ready for a short break over the holiday period. In the case of some of them, their homes were hundreds of miles away and it would be the first time they would have been able to go home to family, friends or sweethearts since starting national service. There was a sense of expectancy as we sat around the communal tables waiting for the motorboat ferry to take us ashore. We listened to the murky river waters slopping against the outside of the ship just below the open porthole.

The ship was some little way off from the actual shore, but everyone looked forward to stepping ashore and making their way home. At the same time, despite the attraction of getting home to Glasgow, Manchester, a farm in Cornwall or a hotel somewhere in 'the big smoke', everybody was beginning to develop a community spirit and learning to live together in the cramped quarters of a naval ship.

For lunch there had been tomato soup, turkey, roast potatoes and stuffing, followed by Christmas pudding and rum. We listened to 'family favourites' on the radio, everyone smoking cigarettes quietly and thinking of home. Finally, the launch came alongside to take us over to the main shipyard. From there we went on to the railway station and said our goodbyes, before going our separate ways. Funnily enough, it wasn't as much of a wrench to go back again after the short break – at least compared with the first time away. Then, when we returned from the Christmas break, we went back to HMS *Raleigh* for the last time and began to widen our experience of naval life.

★★★

For most of the year, the wrens were strictly off-limits – except of course if you were a passably good-looking officer. Then it was different. However, there was one night of the year when the authorities, in their wisdom, relaxed their strict moral stance and gave the ordinary matelots a chance to try their luck. It was the night of the wrens' annual dance. For that night alone it was a case of plying any unsuspecting wrens (if there were any left) with large doses of alcohol and then it was a case of everyone for themselves. Even the patrols and wren officers, who usually kept a close eye on any couples seen in the vicinity of the 'bridge of sighs' that crossed the stream between our camp and the wrens' quarters, relaxed their vigilance. For once the wrens could mix quite happily with the fresh intake of national servicemen and regulars. It made it even more of a challenge that they were outnumbered about three to one.

The authorities may have relaxed their grip a little, but they still took a few precautions. For instance, in order to cool the sailors' ardour and make sure that the events of the evening were cloaked in darkness, the dance night was usually scheduled for sometime in the middle of the winter. Most preparations for the evening's social event started early and by the time darkness closed in, there was a general anticipation of what the sailors fondly imagined would be an orgy. A local band and the camp cinema had been booked in advance and the event was publicised all around the camp.

An hour or so before the dance was due to begin, I was in the mess putting the finishing touches to my smartest uniform when the door burst open and in stalked what appeared to be the purser.

'You,' he called out, as he was entering. 'What do you think you're doing? I'll put you on the duty officer's report.'

He then burst out into drunken chortles and we realised it was Bob Simmons dressed in the purser's uniform. The purser, or 'pusser' as he was generally called, had the rank of a warrant officer, and was in charge of all the administration, stores, food and finances on board a ship. Since he was 'warranted' by the Admiralty, he held a rank equal to an officer and also had a number of privileges. He was usually envied, feared and disliked in equal amounts and was often suspected of having a number of unofficial sidelines to his duties, such as the sale of naval cigarettes and drink for which he was responsible. One of his duties was overseeing distribution of the navy's daily ration of rum on board ships while they were at sea. Also, one of his special privileges was that he answered directly to the captain – something that he jealously guarded. It didn't always make him popular with the other, commissioned officers.

'I found the uniform in the pusser's store,' Bob chortled, 'I think I'll wear it to the dance. It should be a laugh. Anyone coming for a drink in Torpoint before the dance starts?'

It was pretty obvious that he had started already and it took a concerted effort to persuade him that impersonating an officer was not generally a good idea. In the end, when we had all assured him that we weren't going anywhere with him in that get-up, he grudgingly changed back into his own uniform and returned the purser's to the storeroom where he had found it. We set off for the nearest pub and it was only after about an hour's steady drinking that everyone felt able to face a dance floor full of wrens.

Somehow news of the dance had got outside the training camp, and by the time we eventually got back to the packed hall we were greeted by a wall of noise and a scrum of sailors from other ships. Standing on the edge of the jostling, heaving dance floor, we noticed that any pretence at dancing had ceased long ago. I noticed a couple coming towards us, cleaving a path through the crowds. It was Bob, with a half bottle of something in one hand and leading a stocky, blonde-haired girl with the other.

'Haven't you got a girl yet?' he asked in surprise, having to shout to make himself heard above the din. 'Here, have a drink,' and he thrust the bottle into my hand. Then he seemed to remember that he wasn't alone. 'Oh, by the way, meet Yvonne.' He indicated his bulging companion, who was clinging on to him for support.

'Hello,' she shouted, 'who's going to buy me a drink?'

'I'll get you one,' I answered and then added, looking doubtfully at the bottle Bob had handed me, 'as soon as I've finished this. By the way, what is it?'

'Oh, it's fairly harmless,' he told me seriously, 'it's mostly lager, I think, but with a few other things added. Just to give it a bit of flavour, like.'

I took a small sip suspiciously, but it seemed OK, so I drained the rest in a couple of large gulps. I felt the warming effect of the drink all the way down to my stomach, but Bob didn't seem too happy about it.

'Hey, I said have a drink, not finish it off. You'll have to get us all a round in,' and with that he plunged back into the scrum of people and headed for the bar. As we followed, he called back over his shoulder, 'You can meet "Fish".'

I never did discover her real name, but as we got near the bar Bob indicated a large girl standing in front of an admiring group of sailors. She had her head thrown back, a full glass of beer held to her lips and a determined look on her face. I watched in amazement as the level in the glass dropped suddenly, as if someone had pulled a plug out. In a matter of a few seconds she had banged the now empty glass back on the bar.

'What do you think of that?' shouted Bob. 'She can do that all night.'

'That's quite a party trick,' I said, admiringly, 'who is she?'

'I don't know her name,' he admitted, 'but I think she's a nurse in the sick bay.'

I managed to attract a barman's attention and started to order a round of drinks. I just had time to notice that Fish had begun her next pint when someone set off the fire alarm and the lights went out.

There followed what can loosely be described as 'a lot of groping around in the dark', but whatever you called it, there were quite a lot of wrens with red faces afterwards. And of course it was the end of the dance. Following the initial chaos, everyone finally managed to pile out of the hall and into the night air. For a while there were a number of small groups of sailors and wrens standing around wondering what to do, but when the fire brigade arrived and it became obvious that the dance wasn't going to start again any time soon, everyone slowly dispersed. I trudged back to the barracks in disgust, realising that I'd even paid for a round of drinks that I would never see again.

Next morning we were all summoned to the administration block and told to report to the duty officer. As we lined up outside we were all wondering whether one of the wrens had complained, or if the culprit who had set off the alarm had been found. Perhaps there was going to be a group punishment.

Eventually, after about ten minutes, the camp commander appeared round the corner, closely followed by a chief petty officer. They both came to a halt in front of our serried ranks, standing now stiffly to attention. The commander stood grimly with his feet apart and his hands clasped behind his back. He was obviously trying to contain his anger and he kept rising up and down on his toes. All the while the muscles around his jaws were twitching.

'All right,' he almost hissed, 'which one of you threw my bicycle into the static water tank?'

Chapter 5

Shore Leave

At the end of our six months training, the seemingly impossible had been achieved. The rough corners had been knocked off the original group of raw recruits and we were almost in what the navy would have called 'ship-shape'. Even the instructor grudgingly admitted we probably wouldn't be a disgrace to him. It was noticeable that even the original rebel in our group, Phil Roberts, had eventually submitted to the regime. By now he had had his prized hair cut to regulation length, his sideburns shaved off and his Teddy boy outfit discarded in favour of a naval uniform. The navy could never be accused of stinting on dress code and like the rest of us he had plenty from which to choose.

Also, like the rest of us, when he joined he would have been kitted out with a best blue, formal No.1 uniform. Strictly speaking it should only be worn in the northern hemisphere on ceremonial occasions, but apart from the fact that the average matelot didn't attend many ceremonial occasions, it wasn't always clear what to wear and at what times to wear them. Naval etiquette on wear was dictated by a number of different categories and even sub-divisions within those categories.

For instance, the No.1 best uniform was actually a 1A if it was worn by someone who was also both wearing his medals and bearing arms. On the other hand, it was a 1B if he wasn't carrying guns but was wearing medals, and of course it was a 1C if he didn't have either. The regular seamen were given a made-to-measure suit in a proper, tailored cloth, whist we national servicemen had to make do with a much cheaper off-the-shelf variety.

In the case of officers, they would have a No. 2 uniform for wearing on formal mess evenings. Although their uniform was similarly categorised into 2A, B and C, it was more likely that the officer would have been wearing a cummerbund and not a rifle. In fact, it seems that the carrying of arms in the dining room was considered not only unnecessary, but possibly dangerous as well.

Thankfully for us, as well as the more formal uniforms, there was a No. 3 set for all the year round general use, and Nos 4 and 5 shirt and trousers for when we were engaged in any sort of work. Naturally there were white versions of all these for use in the tropics. You couldn't accuse the MoD of being stingy when it came to dress.

So we certainly couldn't complain that we had nothing to wear. The navy even provided us with socks and underwear. All we needed was an excuse to dress up and it was several weeks before we had the first real opportunity. Up until then we had been confined to barracks, but once we had completed the first phase of our training, this ruling was relaxed and discipline was a little less strict. By that time, presumably, those in charge were confident that we would come back again.

For the first time since we had arrived, we could actually walk out of the camp and visit the nearby bright lights of Plymouth. By evening time on the first night we were allowed out, we were all dressed up and ready to go 'ashore'. Look out world, everyone's appearance seemed to shout, here we come!

Naturally, the first thing we had to do was to get drunk and to lose our virginity – in that order, if possible, for those of us who still had a virginity to lose! It wasn't yet the 'swinging sixties', but at least there weren't any concerns about getting AIDS or things like that. There was a risk of catching syphilis or gonorrhoea but a 'dose of clap', as it was known, was considered by many as a kind of badge of honour. Almost the same as the facial cuts and bruises that were proof you were tough enough to get into fights. On the other hand, for those who preferred to be a bit more careful, the navy was thoughtful enough to provide free 'johnnies' at the gatehouse as you left the barracks in the evening!

We caught the bus that ran down to a ferry at Torpoint, crossed the River Tamar and then on the other side caught another bus into Plymouth. Generations of sailors had been convinced that the best pubs and the most beautiful girls were just waiting to welcome them there, so the least we could do was carry on the tradition.

It was still early and so, together with three or four others, I decided to go and see a John Wayne western at the local Odeon cinema. The film was full of cavalry charges and scenes of carnage, so we noisily cheered on the heroes and hissed at the baddies. Halfway through, Taffy Evans, who was sitting next to the aisle at the end of our row, decided to grope the ice cream girl as she got ready for the interval. Unfortunately, what in the dark he had mistakenly taken to be a buxom young girl, turned out to be a large and worldly-wise granny who was probably having a long and tiring day. She promptly hit him on the head with her tray of drinks and in the general rumpus that followed we decided that it was a good time to leave. We hastily got up and made our way outside before someone called the police.

Wandering around, looking for somewhere to eat, we chose a likely-looking café with a large board outside the front door which requested customers: 'Please don't ask the waitress for her measurements; they are 42-26-36, but that's none of your business! And by the way, we would also respectfully remind you that though in God we trust, others must pay cash.'

Intrigued, we went in.

It must have been the waitress's night off, because there was no sign of her. We decided to order fish and chips. Some time later we followed it up with a few drinks in a nearby pub. Then as darkness began to fall, we split up into smaller groups and a few of us made our way up the road and past the NAAFI club on to the long stretch of wide open green known as the Hoe. At the top, overlooking the seawater swimming pool down below the promenade, we could just make out the statue of Drake, which kept a lonely vigil gazing down the length of the 'Sound' and out to the open sea. In the half light, he looked as if was expecting another Armada at any moment –or perhaps he was just trying not to notice what was going on behind him.

All the way up the Hoe, strategically placed streetlights threw a faint glow on the gum-chewing girls, aged from about fourteen upwards, who strolled expectantly in pairs arm-in-arm around the tarmac paths. In hot pursuit were swarms of sailors and Teddy boys. Meanwhile, all the seats in the wooden shelters scattered around at the edges of the green were already fully occupied with writhing bodies.

Because of our lack of local knowledge we had obviously arrived too late to participate in the proceedings. Instead we went off to find another pub. For the rest of the evening, in between drinking nut brown ale and local 'scrumpy', we entertained the regulars in renderings of navy favourite songs including: 'They say that in the navy the biscuits are very fine, but one fell off a table and killed a pal of mine.'

The pub was obviously a local haunt of the navy and everyone in the bar seemed to know the chorus, joining in with 'Oh, I don't want no more of navy life…' and so it went on until last orders and chucking-out time.

We caught the bus to Devonport and walked back towards the ferry. There, as we waited in a hubble, swaying slightly in the evening breeze, Johnny Williams appeared with a wren clutched in each arm. I realised that he had been missing for a large part of the evening. In fact, the two wrens seemed to be supporting him rather than the other way around and we ended up carrying them all on to the last ferry. The two girls promptly sat on our knees.

'My name's Margaret,' said the small, plump wren perched half on my knee and half on Smithy's.

'Where are you from?' I asked.

'Glasgee,' came back the reply. 'Canna ye tell?'

'Yes, I reckoned so. So do I,' I said, trying to sound convincing. 'That deserves a kiss.'

I threw my arms clumsily around her and endeavoured to give her a passionate embrace. Unfortunately, the girls in Glasgow had obviously learnt a thing or two and she was having none of it. There was a short, sharp struggle and I found myself lying on my back, gazing up at the darkened sky.

I decided that the wisest thing would be to stay there for a while, and in any case I was probably too drunk to take an interest in further romantic endeavours. It wasn't until we had started to approach the far bank of the river that I finally struggled to my feet.

I vaguely heard Smithy call 'Come on, let's get to the bus before it's full up' as he leapt clumsily off the ramp. The sound of a splash was quickly followed by a loud stream of profanities as he landed in several inches of water. Evidently the ferry hadn't yet quite reached the far shore.

Luckily the boat had slowed to a crawl and he managed to scramble up the slipway just ahead of it. He stood unhappily waiting for us, the water dripping from his shoes and making large puddles on the ground.

The ferry didn't carry buses and we had to make our way to the nearby terminus where the last two buses were waiting, one of which was for exclusive use by the wrens. Here we had to say goodbye to our two new friends, but not before Johnny had accompanied them on to the bus. It was now crowded with wrens and it took all our efforts to remove him from the loudly cheering bus in order to catch our own transport. Unfortunately, by the time that we had finally managed to prise him off, it was only to see our own bus disappearing into the distance. It was the last one that night. We calculated that we only had half an hour to get back to the barracks before our shore leave ran out at midnight and as the camp was nearly a mile away, we started to break into a shambling sort of run towards it. The consequences of not returning back in time on the first night out didn't bear thinking about.

We made it to the gates with two minutes to spare and wended our way as quietly as possible past the guardhouse and the sentry on duty. Just in time, we remembered to throw a passable salute in the general direction of the flagpole – though Jimmy's arm needed a bit of assistance. Forgetting to salute the flag, or colours, was a serious misdemeanour in the forces and was particularly so in the navy. There you were expected to show your respect for the monarch by saluting every time you boarded a ship – although in this case the ship was standing on dry land and the gates didn't actually lead on to a proper quarterdeck. To do it properly, the salute had to be made with the right hand, holding the fingers together and the palm facing downwards and at the same time the forefinger should be touching the right eyebrow. In theory we ought to have come to attention as well, but by this time we weren't remembering any of the niceties.

We managed to reach the mess without being challenged and reckoned that our troubles were over. Then we discovered that Johnny had disappeared again. Someone remembered seeing him veering off in the direction of the wrens' quarters and he had been telling anyone who bothered to listen that he had forgotten to kiss Margaret goodnight. Next day he was up on a charge for being found wandering around their camp, opening doors and calling out her name. What was worse, he reckoned that he had never even found her!

Chapter 6

A Ship Named *Cleo*

There was one last ceremony to perform before we would finally be able to leave HMS *Raleigh* and get down to the task of defending the realm. It had become a tradition that before any recruits finally 'passed out' from the barracks, to complete their active service elsewhere, they received a robust send-off from some of the newer trainees. We had got a tip-off of what was likely to happen, so it wasn't entirely unexpected. We had been told by one of the 'regulars' at the barracks that something of the sort often occurred when a group was about to leave and that if there was to be a visit, it would generally take place at night time after lights out. By then only the blue pilot light was lit in each mess and the corridor lights were dimmed. The way they described it, it all sounded a bit public school, with knotted towels and stink bombs.

Sure enough, a couple of nights later, soon after lights out, the attack came. Since we had been prepared for it beforehand, we didn't have much difficulty in repelling the raiders. We hadn't bargained for the greased floor just outside the mess, but all-in-all we thought things could have turned out far worse. Even so, reprisals were still called for, and a couple of days later when we heard that those responsible were boasting of their success, we naturally had to retaliate. It was still only meant to be a fairly low-key, token raid. Just rushing through the mess and tipping a few sleeping bodies out of their beds, letting off a couple of fire extinguishers and then making a quick withdrawal. But unfortunately, they also somehow seemed to have got wind of what we had planned.

Inevitably when you have so many youngsters cooped up together for weeks on end, unable to go home at night to see their families or just get out and let off some steam, it was bound to get a bit out of hand. Added to that, one or two saw it as a way to get back at authority. They were probably bordering on being 'tearaways' anyway in civvy street, and they resented having to do national service. Being 'called up' wasn't exactly what they had in mind. Whatever the reason, the evening didn't turn out quite as planned.

We got into their mess all right, tipped the first few beds over and pulled the bedclothes off others. But, as we turned back for the door, we found that it was impossible to be sure who was trying to get out of the darkened room and who belonged there. All you could make out was a mass of struggling bodies and whirling, knotted towels. Someone started using their fists and the sound of blows and shouting could be heard above the general din. The scrap really started in earnest then!

Half the people in our group concentrated on fighting-off the counter-attack (which by now had spilled out into the corridor), whilst another contingent went round to the back of the building and entered through the rear door, which opened directly into the road. Soon, together with the struggling figures, the area was a jumbled mass of overturned beds and lockers. Bedclothes and personal effects were strewn everywhere. There was even a barrier of upturned beds and lockers just inside the door, from behind which came a hail of boots, shoes and any other handy missiles.

It was about then that someone noticed the row of neatly rolled and tied oilskins hanging up in the corridor just outside the mess door. The first deftly aimed cylinder of rolled oilskin smashed one of the overhead lights and was quickly followed by a fusillade of further projectiles. One of them hit a defender who was sitting up on the overhead rafter busy throwing books at us. With a cry of pain he fell off and on to the struggling figures below. At the same time someone threw a boot aimlessly at the heaving mass and there was a clang as the studs rang against a radiator before it fell to rest at my feet. Without thinking, I filled it with water from the nearby fire bucket hanging on the wall and hurled it back into the darkened room. It landed against the side of the barricade and showered water over the defenders. It was the signal for water-filled articles to be hurled everywhere – soon to be followed by the half-filled fire buckets themselves. Pools of water started spreading across the floor and under the overturned beds.

In the end, there wasn't anything left to throw and by that time the attack had begun to fizzle out anyway. The fighting had stopped and everyone began to realise that what had started as a 'friendly' raid had got well and truly out of hand. A sheepish silence was quickly followed by feverish activity. There was less than an hour before rounds were due.

In the subdued illumination of the night-light we saw that the room was a shambles of water-soaked bedding and clothes, boots and oilskins. Beds and lockers were upturned in the pools of water, together with the tables and chairs and other items that had been used in the barricade. Rather shamefacedly, we agreed to help clear up the worst of the mess before we slunk back to our own barracks.

By the time the duty officer made his rounds of the area after midnight, some semblance of normality had been restored and every bed appeared to contain a sleeping occupant. Although we heard later that he nearly slipped on the wet floor as he passed through the mess and along its hastily re-formed row of beds and lockers, he carried on by and said nothing. It still took most of the next night to sort out the bedclothes, clothing and personal effects, then restore them to their rightful owners. By the time the divisional officer's fortnightly kit inspection took place three days later, peace had been restored again. The night's mayhem seemed to have passed off without any serious comebacks.

★★★

I had mistakenly expected that once I completed basic training I would be assigned to a permanent position for the remainder of my service, but for a while I was given a series of postings that seemed designed to show just how humdrum life in the peacetime navy could be. I began to get the impression that the navy didn't quite know what to do with me next.

The first move saw me travelling eastwards along the coast to end up at Portsmouth, close to where I had gone before for my assessment as officer material. The twin ships HMS *Cleopatra* and HMS *Dido* lay alongside each other at anchor in midstream between Gosport and Pompey – the name by which Portsmouth was better known in the navy. The ships were two of the oldest cruisers left in service, held together by barnacles on the outside and the many layers of oil, paint and whitewash on the inside. Typical 'rust buckets' as the Americans would have euphemistically called them.

I seemed to be one of the few national servicemen located there. Everyone else had been in the forces for years and by now they were street-, or navy-wise. For old hands and newcomers alike though, the day-to-day life was fairly uneventful and most of the crew looked upon this term of duty as nothing short of a holiday. Four hours on watch was followed by four off, for a full twenty-four hours. Then twenty-four hours off duty. Except for assembling or 'falling-in' for 'divisions' under the eagle eye of the divisional officer, Lieutenant Commander Davies, we were left pretty much to ourselves.

Our mess was on *Cleo*, with the toilets or 'heads' located on the deck above. Meanwhile, for some reason our bathrooms were on *Dido*, its twin ship. And as with the heads in most ships, they were not designed for any sort of privacy, with only 3ft-high partitions separating the cubicles. The only advantage seemed to be that it made conversation with the next-door occupant an easy matter.

On one of my visits I noticed that someone had written a warning on the door:

> 'It's no good standing on this seat,
> the crabs in here can jump three feet.'

While another piece of toilet prose in the adjoining cubicle included the belief that 'the Petty Officer is queer', to which someone else had added whimsically, if rather blasphemously, 'thank God'.

The two cruisers weren't strictly 'mothballed', but were kept on reserve and ticking over so that they could, if necessary, be put into active service at a few days notice. Consequently, once a year the Reserve Admiral of the Fleet came on board to carry out an official inspection. This provided the navy with an excuse to clear the fish and the seaweed from the traps in the bilges and to whitewash every dirty or oily pipe in the ship – irrespective of its purpose or proper colour coding. The Admiral's visits could always be mapped by the alternate oil and whitewash layers which covered everything. His visits were also an excuse to cover all the scrap bins and dirty clothes baskets with tarpaulins and try instead to make them look like vital items of equipment. Any compartments which probably wouldn't stand up to inspection were locked, 'danger' notices hung outside the door and the keys promptly lost.

It was during my short tour of duty on the *Cleopatra* that I learnt the old forces adage, 'If it moves, salute it and if it doesn't, then whitewash it!' This appeared to be one of the navy's ten key rules and over the next year or two I put it into practice on more than one occasion.

The Admiral's last visit had thankfully passed without incident and we lay on our backs sunbathing on the fire deck beneath the long, grey, steel barrels of the 4.5in guns. I lazily watched the feathery white vapour trails of a squadron of aircraft far above us as they slowly crossed the pale blue sky in perfectly parallel lines. As they neared the horizon, they began to criss-cross like a tangled ball of wool in what seemed like an aerial battle taking place far away. It could have been in another world as far as we were concerned.

'This is my idea of watch keeping,' murmured Pete Robertson, who lay stretched out nearby. I had to agree with him. As 'stokers' or, to be more accurate, as MEs or mechanical engineers, our responsibility was to look after all the ship's machinery. But there wasn't a lot to do, since there were very few machines operating on board whilst the two cruisers were on stand-by. The ships' generators, refrigerators and pumps for the heads and bilges were about the only ones operating and they practically ran themselves. Perhaps the CO_2 refrigerator control would need bringing down a few degrees once every five or six hours and nobody saw any reason to touch it or watch over it in the meantime. During the night we could even sling our hammocks and safely leave everything alone for the whole of the watch.

None of us actually risked the wrath of the ever-watchful chief by not being on duty when he made his rounds, but if you kept out of trouble and appeared to be on watch at the right times it was not what you would call an onerous job.

'What were you in civvy street, Pete?' I enquired idly.

'Fuckin' 'appy,' he replied after a moment's thought.

I turned on one side and watched the small, brightly coloured yachts and white sails dotted around the wide estuary as they weaved in and out of the dirty grey mud flats and grassy banks. They would be covered by water at each succeeding tide and you had to know the estuary in order to navigate safely. The almost naked figure of Smithy clambered up from the row of sunbathing bodies and began to idly unscrew loose nuts from the thousands of bolts that, together with rivets, held together the gun turret plates. Going to the side of the ship, he began to hurl them at the seagulls wheeling overhead and occasionally swooping down to grab floating scraps of food in the water.

'Ah, got one of the bastards,' he cried out triumphantly as the bird faltered in mid-flight, then dropped a couple of feet, recovered and flew on again. Smithy continued throwing nuts and bolts at seagulls for a few moments and then, tiring of his efforts, turned and lay down again alongside a group who had raised enough energy to play poker. 'The little bastards must see them coming,' he explained disgustedly.

He was silent for a while, as if in contemplation, and then said, to no one in particular, 'Did you hear about the fight outside the Castle last night?' The Blenheim Castle was a Gosport pub just off the main road into town, with a reputation for being pretty lively – particularly on a Saturday night.

'Yeah,' he continued, as no one bothered to answer, 'when I came out of the Castle after a few drinks like, there were these Teddy boys kicking hell out of a PO on the ground. I got a bit mad when I saw some matelots standing around at a bus stop across the road not bothering to help 'im, so I rush in and grab one of the blokes and throw 'im in the road. Then the little bloke who was kicking the shit out of the PO comes over and tries to butt me. He was only a skinny bloke and when I kicked 'im, he went down straight away. Then I got a good punch in the face on the other bloke and they had had enough. Then this woman has the cheek to go on at me for fighting and the PO is still lying on the pavement. I was too puffed to pick him up, but some of the other guys helped him up and said he was OK. So I legged it before the law came.'

It was a long speech and seemed to exhaust him. 'It was a good scrap while it lasted,' he added after a while and he turned to me, as if for support.

'Yes,' I said, trying to sound enthusiastic, 'it sounds like it.'

He went quiet for a minute, deep in thought. Then, he seemed to remember [using language that was not unusual amongst servicemen at the time]:

'One of the best scraps I ever had was out in Colombo, when I got my nose busted by a wog. See, I was up on one of the tea plantations, knocking off this party up there. She was married see, but her husband was away. Only about twenty years old she was and a nice piece of skirt too. I was having a drink with her one night in a local pub, when this drunken wog comes over and starts trying to barge in. Put his arm round her and tried to chat her up, even with me there. Well, out there a wog isn't allowed to touch a white girl see, and she'd only just come out of hospital from an operation as well. So I let fly and let him have one. Of course, all of the others there were his mates weren't they and two others came over to join in and one of them tried to kick me in the goolies.

Well you know these wogs. Give them one good slap and they've usually had enough. And I was doing all right see. I'd planted two of them, and I'd got my back to the bar so they couldn't get behind me. Then, wham – the barman cracks me on the head with a bottle and as I goes down one of them busts my nose in with his boot and I go out like a light. Next day, I sees a doc out there and he reckoned I needed an op' on it when I got home. Cos the bones are crushed, see, and they've set it all wrong. But I reckon I'll wait 'til I'm due some leave and then 'ave the op a couple of weeks beforehand. That way, I should end up with about a month off, what with convalescent leave an' all.' Although his choice of language left a lot to be desired, I got the general picture.

He seemed to have the system pretty well 'sussed out' as they said. I was given plenty of free advice about 'beating the system' on my tour of duty at HMS *Cleopatra*. One idea that I wasn't actually able to verify was that I should have got married just before I was called up. Then, if I had quickly rented a house and bought some expensive items like a car or furniture and paid for them on hire purchase over a two-year period, I was assured that I wouldn't actually have to pay for them myself. According to my confidant at the time, the navy was responsible for the instalments whilst I was in their service. Apparently the theory was that by the time I had completed my two years service, the navy would have paid for it all. It sounded like an ingenious scam to me, except that I was fairly sure it would involve a divorce and a writ for deception afterwards.

Finding ways to defeat the authorities had become a full-time occupation with a lot of the crew I met on HMS *Cleopatra*. It was on that tour of duty that I met 'Taffy' Roberts, who was busily trying to work his passage out of the forces. It appeared that all Welshmen were automatically called Taffy in the navy – or anywhere else, for that matter!

He had left school at fifteen and spent the next couple of years learning the haircutting business as a barber's apprentice in Swansea. Then, getting restless feet, thinking he might pursue his trade in some more exotic surroundings, and against his parents' advice, he went along to the naval recruitment office.

'I want to be a hairdresser in the navy,' he informed the bored-looking clerk behind the desk. It didn't seem to cause a great deal of interest.

'You do, do you?' the other rejoined, and glanced out of the window at a passer-by.

'Yes, you see hairdressing is my trade, and I want to see the world,' explained Taffy with Welsh determination.

The man behind the desk had had a bad day and he was also possessed of a perverse sense of humour. 'We don't have any vacancies for hairdressers at the moment,' he said, 'but you could join the engineering branch and work your way up.' So Taffy did.

When I met Taffy on the *Cleo*, he'd been in for a year and had been desperately trying to get out of being a stoker. He was partly resigned to having to see out his minimum service, but in the meantime he took a wilful pleasure in dealing out horrible haircuts to any unsuspecting newcomer to the ship who had seen his haircutting tools and heard of Taffy's skills.

He finally got the discharge he sought, but it took a party thrown at short notice on board a ship in Hong Kong by some high-ranking officials to get it for him. The first lieutenant of the ship, who had been put in charge of all the arrangements, had realised just before it was due to start, that after a month at sea, he was looking a bit scruffy on top. There was no time to get ashore and they didn't have a barber on board. Something had to be done quickly, and hearing about Taffy's skills, he didn't hesitate or stop to consider the consequences. Taffy was summonsed to the Jimmy's office 'at the rush', and ordered to help out. Too late, he realised his mistake.

When the guests arrived, they were of course sorry to hear that the first officer was indisposed and in bed with an unknown malaise. Taffy got his release soon afterwards. They say he now works happily at his own barbers shop in Merthyr Tydfil, where the miners queued up to get one of his special 'stoker's cuts'.

Glancing at my wristwatch, I realised that I just had time to change before I was due to go on duty. So, unable to stay and discuss Pete's means of getting extra time off – albeit, I thought, a rather painful one – I hurriedly got to my feet and went down below to our mess.

★★★

Perhaps it was because we didn't have any real wars to fight that the Admiralty was keen to have mock ones. On the other hand, it could have been because we needed the practice. Whatever the reason, every so often the ship was ordered to have what became known as a 'special drill'.

We were relaxing in the mess one morning after the normal tidying up duties when over the tannoy, with a flourish of bugles, it was announced that we would be having a special drill and that as part of this, the ship alongside (which happened to be our sister cruiser HMS *Dido*) had been disabled by enemy attack which set it on fire. As a result, it had to be evacuated.

The next few minutes were not quite the snappy reaction of a well-oiled machine that the organisers had hoped for. Our ship was soon 'invaded' by swarms of seamen and marines from the distressed *Dido* and the situation became more than a little confused. It didn't help when it was decided that although the *Dido* was on fire, unofficially it would be better to ensure that the vital auxiliary machinery such as generators, refrigerating plants and bilge pumps were kept running. This meant that a number of stokers from *Cleopatra*, including myself, were ordered to go over and replace those who would have normally been on duty there. It rather defeated the object of the exercise since we naturally presumed that we would be automatically counted out of the exercise. Or alternatively we would be considered as dead. In any case, we reasoned that they wouldn't expect us to take any further notice of tannoy announcements.

So when, soon afterwards, another call came over the system announcing that an atom bomb had fallen some miles away, it was largely ignored. No one thought to close the metal shutters (or 'scuttles' as they were called), over the portholes. Consequently, much of the ship would presumably have been filled with radioactive dust.

Down below where we were working, a short, fat CPO had appeared in the doorway. He took off his gas mask and mopped his sweating brow. 'For God's sake close those scuttles before an officer sees them,' he gasped, 'don't you know that an atom bomb has exploded?'

Jeers and shouts of scorn came from all sides.

'Ah, go on Chief, someone's been 'avin' you on. Here, 'ave a drink.' An open can of beer was passed over to him.

'Come on,' he insisted, as he tried to talk and take a drink at the same time. 'Get them closed, or you'll all be on captain's defaulters tomorrow.'

Hoots of laughter followed his threat. He was known to have difficulty in maintaining authority and was regarded by the crew as a soft touch.

'Can't be done Chief, the lockers are in the way. Have another drink,' we called after him as, looking somewhat embarrassed, he turned and hurried out. The officer who came round later to inspect the area got quite upset, until of course he too found out that the scuttles really couldn't be closed properly, due to the pile of lockers in the way.

Outside meanwhile, a couple of stokers had been blissfully unaware of what was going on around them and had continued working on the engine of the reserve fleet admiral's launch, which was drawn up alongside. They were extremely surprised to see a figure wearing a white decontamination suit and gas mask topped off with an officer's cap appear over the railings high above them. They were even more surprised when the gas mask was removed and the figure began to shout down at them.

'You bloody fools,' he yelled, 'what do you think you are doing down there. Don't you know that there is a drill going on, and the whole place is flooded with radioactive dust? If the exercise was the real thing, you'd both be dead by now.'

The two stokers looked at one another and then upwards, realising now that the head belonged to their lieutenant. 'Yes sir,' one of them called upwards, and then added as an afterthought, 'Er ... is it all right if we carry on now sir?'

'You're both dead, do you understand?' and the head disappeared. A few seconds later, it reappeared. 'And report to me in the morning,' it called down.

Later that afternoon, the captain announced over the tannoy that the danger had passed. Gas masks were removed, doors, hatches and scuttles opened and hoses unrolled to wash down the ship and remove the imaginary radioactive dust. The result was the removal of a great deal of accumulated dirt, together with the soaking of an off-duty member of the crew who was sunbathing surreptitiously out of sight in one of the gun turrets. We sailed back to our berth in the estuary and the order was given to drop anchor.

The afternoon's 'entertainment' concluded with a whaler boat race between the stokers and the shipwrights; which the stokers lost miserably! Evening time started to draw in and as we were finishing up and putting everything away, a police launch and motor-driven pontoon carrying six heavy trucks appeared. Unfortunately, nobody seemed to know what part they were supposed to play in the exercise and we were still trying to work it out when, a few days later, I got instructions to transfer once again – this time to a berth not very far away.

CHAPTER 7

HIGHLAND FLING

Although HMS *Theseus* was officially an aircraft carrier, she had lost all her aircraft long ago. When I joined her, she was tied up alongside the quay at Portsmouth dockyard, just down the estuary from where I had been earlier. I found out that she had a reputation with all who sailed in her as an unlucky ship. After a while I began to see why.

The keel had been laid down in Glasgow's Govan shipyard early in 1943, but she wasn't finally launched until the end of the following year and commissioned in 1946. She displaced more than 13,000 tons, had a speed of 25 knots and could carry nearly fifty aircraft. In the end she wasn't commissioned in time to see any active service in the Second World War as was originally intended. The Admiralty decided that although the ship had originally been designed for an offensive support role, she would serve instead for training purposes. The navy could use her for practising taking off, flying and landing exercises. So, in 1947 she went on her first long voyage to the Far East, sailing through the Mediterranean and the Suez Canal before going on to Singapore, Australia and New Zealand. It was during this trip that she first got the reputation for courting disaster; a reputation that stayed with her until the end.

The first sign of trouble occurred when two seamen became so overcome by the welcoming reception in Melbourne that they promptly tried to jump ship. Later, there were to be a whole series of mishaps on that first trip, including a mid-air collision and several ditched aircraft resulting from ill-judged landings. Finally, in July, when they were off the coast of Australia, an aircraft crash-landed on the deck, somehow missed the arrestor cable and smashed instead into two parked aircraft; killing a watching mechanic, injuring others and causing a great deal of damage. It so happened that the captain's wife was staying and sleeping on board at the time. Since this was generally considered to be very bad luck for a ship, a legend was born.

The tour of duty was completed without further serious mishap and *Theseus* eventually left Singapore and returned home. Soon the Korean War broke out. It seemed like a lucky break for the Admiralty but not for everyone else. There was a period of feverish activity to equip the ship for service and the loss of lives and the damaged planes of the 1947 trip were quietly forgotten. Nevertheless, the legend lived on. Soon after she had arrived off Korea and started her support operations, the steam catapult stopped working and as a result they were unable to arm the planes, since they would then have been too heavy to take off. For a while the *Theseus* was restricted to reconnaissance work only.

For a while, things took a turn for the better and their fortunes began to look up. They not only performed the air strikes with great success, but the *Theseus* was awarded the Boyd Trophy for both the pilots and aircrew when they completed over 1,000 accident-free landings. The whole crew was commended for performing with courage and profes-sionalism throughout the conflict.

Unfortunately, however, it was not to be the end of their troubles. Apart from the inevitable tragedies of war, a war which was being carried out in wintertime and in atrocious conditions, a series of unrelated accidents followed. Planes and pilots crashed on several occasions, some landing in the sea for no apparent reason and others whilst landing. Bad luck seemed to dog her activities! In one incident as a Firefly aircraft was coming in to land, its guns started to fire by accident and one of its bul-lets killed a petty officer. For some reason it was the accidents that got remembered and not the heroism. On her last role of duty, the *Theseus* took an active part in supporting the ill-fated Suez Canal conflict.

The ship was finally put on reserve for most of the 1950s, but then taken into service again and given a refit instead. When I joined her, the planes had gone long ago and the hangars were converted into mess decks. As I went on board I realised that the refit hadn't yet been fin-ished. It had already lasted at least a couple of months and there was no sign of it being completed in another couple.

Nearby, in a dry dock, was her sister ship, HMS *Illustrious*. She had been there for over ten years and was now known to all those who worked on her as the ship that was never completed. She had originally been laid down at the end of the war but before she had been finished, the Admiralty concluded that the navigation equipment was out of date. So they replaced it all. Next it was decreed that they must fit more up-to-date armaments and then later a new, re-designed bridge was fitted. When I got there, the flight deck had been replaced with the latest angled version but unfortunately, because of all the extra weight, the ship would now need new, more powerful engines. Nobody had yet dared to work out what it had all cost!

On board *Theseus* everything was in disorder. We were due to sail in a week's time for sea trials, but there was little chance of that. The most obvious sign of slippage was on the flight deck, which was littered everywhere with cables, drums, spars and tools. In the machinery rooms, it felt as if the army of 'dockyard maties' in brown overalls outnumbered the naval personnel by two to one. None of the machinery was in working order and bits and pieces of compressors, evaporators and engines lay everywhere. Decks were awash with coils of wire, hoses, pipes, lagging and pumps. And in spite of there being electricians everywhere, only half the lights were working. The bilges, which were nearly 2ft deep in oil and water, were full of replaced bits of machinery and assorted tools which had dropped there from above. Anyone who ventured down below risked life and limb from falling steel.

Sailors are a superstitious lot and everyone was convinced that the *Theseus* was a doomed ship. Nearly every time she docked (and sometimes when she just went to sea) someone got killed. On the last trip, seven seamen had lost their lives when one of the ship's whaler boats had capsized. Then, when she had put into port for the refit, one of the dockyard employees was nearly decapitated on the flight deck by a whipping, broken cable.

We spent the next few weeks trying to clear up the mess and restore some sort of order to the ship. The sailing was rescheduled for two weeks time, but at the end of the two weeks we were still nowhere near ready. They put the sailing date back yet again for another two weeks. In the meantime, a Canadian aircraft carrier arrived nearby and there was the usual round of brawls, drinking challenges, missing persons and broken romances around Portsmouth.

Finally the time came for us to depart and, to the accompaniment of the marine band and the cheers of friends and families gathered on the dockside or along the foreshore and nearby piers, we cast off. It was mid-morning on a bright, sunny, early June day. The crew were all lined up on the flight deck and we watched as first the dockyard and then the narrow entrance to the harbour slipped slowly past us. The shoreline at Southsea disappeared and after a while we rounded the Isle of Wight and headed out into the English Channel. Two days later, after having criss-crossed the North Sea undertaking speed trials, we managed to reach the Moray Firth, but not before we had nearly run into an oil tanker in the dark when the radar broke down. Once there we hastily sought shelter at Invergordon, situated beyond the narrow straits of the Cromarty, before anything else could befall us.

The town of Invergordon lies on the shores of a small inland sea over-looked by the Scottish Highlands. Apart from the vast number of large oil tanks built slap-bang in the middle, there wasn't much to distinguish the town from the many other similar seaside ports which were dotted along the coast. Apart from a peripheral oil industry, the main income came from the navy, and the NAAFI was one of the biggest buildings in town. It also boasted one cinema, three pubs and three or four temperance hotels to serve the tourist and oil trades. There seemed to be an equal number of fish and chip shops.

Before the navy had discovered its deep-water harbour and had started to anchor its ships there, the town hardly existed. According to the locals, work had been so scarce at one time that an ex-governor of India who lived nearby and owned a large estate, had tried to solve the unemployment problem by employing the locals to build a monument on top of the nearby mountain. According to local folklore, he paid the town's residents a penny for every stone they carried to the top with which to build it.

Just before we got there, the American air force had finally evacuated the local airfield. They had been there for the last couple of decades and when we arrived, it looked as if every girl in town over the age of about fifteen was wheeling a pram and chewing gum. You couldn't say that we were the most welcome of visitors either, and we were instructed that for the next ten days we had to make every effort to keep out of trouble. The only thing to do seemed to be to pursue innocuous pursuits such as climbing, playing football and riding 'pussers red' bicycles around the area.

The peace in town lasted for about eight days and then Stuart Black, one of the stokers who had been on HMS *Cleo* at the same time as I was, couldn't keep it up any longer. One day, he went ashore without his station card, got roaring drunk and picked a fight with the navy patrol. He was promptly carried back on board and taken to the RPO's office.

Stuart sank to the floor in one corner, happily singing to himself while they waited for the RPO to appear. Tiring of his singing, Stuart started to reminisce loudly to the patrolmen.

'Och, that wee blonde had it all,' he said, to nobody in particular. 'And she'd kept it all that time, just for Stu.'

'What's your name?' asked the RPO, who had arrived in the meantime and was in no mood for friendly banter. He was also thinking that he could have been in his bed by now if it hadn't been for drunks like Stuart.

'Don't you know who I am?' exclaimed Stuart, struggling to his feet and waving his finger under the RPO's nose as sternly as he could manage. 'I'm the captain,' he said, and collapsed back on to the floor.

The RPO wasn't impressed and neither was the captain when Stuart came up before him on a charge the next morning. The upshot was that he got drafted back to base and they sent him off to take the train back to Chatham barracks. No one was very surprised when it took him three days to arrive, having dropped off at Glasgow to call in at home. For that transgression he was given an additional twenty-one days stoppage of leave.

Some time later, he apparently decided to volunteer for service in submarines and I bumped into him again in the headquarters at HMS *Dolphin*. But all that was a bit later. Meanwhile, we had another incident on board, this time involving the ship's flag or 'colours'.

When a ship is anchored in port, it's both a tradition and a regulation that at approximately five minutes before sunset, the captain gives the order 'first call to colours'. Sometimes a bugle call known as a 'first call' is sounded instead over the tannoy system. In addition, on ceremonial occasions, for instance, the guard of the day and the naval band are paraded on deck. Then, either the bugle call 'attention' is sounded or a long blast is given on the ship's whistle. As the sun is setting, the word is passed to 'execute', and the National Anthem or the bugle call 'retreat' is played. The duty seaman starts to lower the ensign (or the 'colours') at the start of the music and continues to lower the flag slowly whilst it is playing. The knack is to time it just right so that it's fully lowered as the last note sounds. On board ship, the Union Jack is lowered simultan-eously from the flag pole.

I had learnt early on that it was a long-established and solemn cer-emony, not to be taken light-heartedly. All naval personnel who are within earshot are expected to turn towards the ensign and salute during the playing of the 'retreat' or the National Anthem. Then, when the ceremony is finished, the bugle call for 'carry on' is sounded. Sometimes three blasts are given on the ship's whistle instead. Of course, to make things a bit more complicated, none of this applies to ships that are 'under way'. When ships are at sea, their flags are flown only during daylight hours and then only under conditions as specified in Navy Regulations, such as cruising near land, when falling in with other ships, coming to anchor, or in combat, etc. That, at least, is the theory, but on that particular evening there was something of a break from tradition.

Piped over the tannoy from the back of the ship (normally reserved for the lowering of the colours) came the announcement: 'There will be no moon tonight, but tomorrow there will be a small moon for CPOs and POs only.'

To say that the ship's crew were a little surprised would have been putting it mildly! We all stared in astonishment as the tannoy died away into silence. It sounded like a hoax, but no one was sure. Soon we had raised the anchor and, on a full tide, we had managed to float off the col-lection of discarded beer cans underneath the ship. By the next day it was all round the ship that the seaman responsible for the prank had been put on a charge. Since it was about the only entertainment we had had on that trip, we all thought it was a bit harsh under the circumstances.

By the time we had got back home I had already decided it was time to get away from the rather regimented and (to my mind, anyway) anachronistic regime of big ships. I had taken to heart the advice of a sailor that I had met just before joining *Theseus*: 'You don't want to get on one of them aircraft carriers,' he had told me succinctly, if somewhat crudely. 'Big bastards, they are. You could put a destroyer inside one of them buggers and it would be like a fly in a pisspot. I bide the time we was on the *Warrior*,' he continued, rather unconvincingly. 'We'd been at sea about three weeks before we found the captain, as oiled as a coot, wandering along a corridor on 'C' deck looking for his own cabin.'

By then I had begun to understand what he had meant about big ships, so I volunteered for service in submarines instead.

CHAPTER 8

ESCAPE

Rather wisely the Admiralty had decided not to let anyone loose in a submarine before they had undergone some basic safety checks and training. That applied to everyone – national serviceman or not. First they had to be sure that you didn't suffer from claustrophobia (which was a sensible precaution in view of the confined spaces in a submarine) and also that your ear drums could withstand the occasional high pressures that might be encountered in service. Then, if the worst should happen and there was an accident at sea, as an added precaution all submarine crew had to be trained in how to escape from a stricken boat.

And so, soon after getting back to Portsmouth from my Scottish outing, I caught the naval ferry across the short stretch of water to the other side of the harbour and from there to the nearby naval base at Haslar. It was here that HMS *Dolphin* served as both the submarine base and its headquarters. As soon as I arrived, I was directed to the newly built Submarine Escape Training Tank.

'Och, it's the tank you want,' the duty admin petty officer told us. 'You canna miss it.' And he was right.

The tall, grey, elongated, square-shaped steel tower dominated the skyline over on the west side of Portsmouth harbour mouth, the rather plain exterior broken by a vertical line of windows marking the different floors. It widened out towards the top, nearly 200ft overhead, making it look top heavy. Inside I discovered that it held an inverted 100ft-high, 15ft-diameter steel tube built over the mock-up of a submarine control room and filled with over 150,000 gallons of water. Stairs inside the building ran up to a floor at the top of the water-filled tube, where there was a large training and instruction room surrounding its open end. The centre was just known as 'the tower', and was a name spoken with some respect and pride by those undergoing submarine escape training.

We were a group of about ten new recruits to submarines. I soon discovered that I was the only national serviceman amongst them. We filed into the changing rooms located on the ground floor and we all changed out of our uniforms and into swimming trunks, not quite knowing what to expect. It didn't help to see that the chief instructor who entered the changing rooms shortly afterwards had lost most of his hair. An occupational hazard, we learned, that was the result of regular, daily immersion in the pools.

'Right, gather round,' he barked out by way of introduction, not bothering to introduce himself. 'Don't make any plans for the next couple of days. You'll be doing some training in the basic methods of escape.' He paused for a moment to let that sink in and then managed a grin. 'Of course that means from submarines, not from the navy,' he added. 'We don't teach that here. There's nothing very difficult in what we do, so you might even enjoy it. Some of you,' he went on, 'have probably heard stories of hatches being clipped down from the outside so that nobody can desert. In that case, you could ask, what the hell is the use of you learning escape training. Well as a matter of fact, during the last war they did screw down the hatches in combat to stop them being blown in by depth charges. That was so you could dive deep and avoid the enemy, see. As a matter of fact,' he said, and his face broke into what I took to be a smile, 'if the hatches were blown in, you wouldn't have to worry about escape training anyway, would you?'

'Cheerful bastard, isn't he?' I heard someone behind me murmur.

Seemingly undeterred, he continued with his welcoming speech. 'I am happy to be able to tell you that we aren't at war, and after completing this training, you'll know how to get out safely from either the hatches or the conning tower – assuming, of course, you remembered to close the bulkhead doors in the first place! We give you the benefit of this training because it has saved a lot of lives already and it will no doubt save lots more. These days you can escape from almost any depth, with or without breathing apparatus or life jackets, using what we call free ascent. The theory is that it's better to risk drowning while trying to escape than it is to suffocate 500ft down, waiting for someone to come and find you. First we'll get used to some pressure changes and we'll try using the Davis breathing apparatus. There's only a few subs that still have them fitted, but for now you might as well learn how to handle it. We'll use the small pool here on the ground floor today, and then if everything is going OK, we'll move on to the main tank tomorrow. Then we will go through the more regular free escape procedures.'

He led us to the side of a small, 15ft-deep tank of water where, from a table standing at the side, we each collected a pair of goggles, a nose clip and a set of breathing gear. The so-called Davis set seemed to consist of two rubber bags that strapped around the chest, together with a cylinder of oxygen and a breathing mask which was attached by a hose to one of the bags. He demonstrated how this bag could be filled from the cylinder by briefly opening the integral shut-off valve. The air inside could then be breathed through the attached mask. Any CO_2 breathed out was absorbed chemically in a filter. The second bag could be inflated by breaking a small container located inside. This then gave the wearer some additional buoyancy and helped him reach the surface more quickly.

Once we had had it demonstrated a couple of times, we donned the Davis gear and put on our chosen pair of goggles. Then with a nose clip in place, everyone tentatively opened and shut the regulator valve to let some oxygen into the bag around their chest. I put in my mouthpiece to start breathing – and pulled it off again hastily as I started to gasp and splutter. It turned out that I wasn't the only one, as we all struggled to adapt from our more normal habit of breathing through the nose.

After a while, and with a little practice, we learned the knack of breathing in and out through our mouths. Then, after a few more test runs, and breathing all the while from the mouthpieces, we felt confident enough to climb gingerly down the ladders on the side of the tank and into the water. Gaining confidence all the while, we carried on down – albeit with a safety line attached at our belts and the other end held by an instructor!

The instructors gave two tugs on the line to check if we were all right so far and, as agreed beforehand, we gave a couple of tugs back in confirmation. Even at that depth we could feel the increased pressure on our ears. So as we had been shown, we used one hand to squeeze off the breathing hose and, with the other hand over the nose clip to back it up, made as if to snort down our noses. This immediately helped to clear our ears since, by equalising the pressures on the inside and outside of the eardrums, any pain went away. So far, so good, I thought, as I climbed further down the ladder and finally stood on the bottom.

Two more pulls came on the line at my belt and I gave two energetic jerks back. I glanced upward and was just in time to see the tracksuit-clad instructor at the end of my line who, like the others, had been leaning forward to watch progress below, tip forward and land with a splash on the surface of the pool.

I thought it was probably time to go back up to the surface, where I suspected my reception wasn't going to be very welcoming. I broke the small container inside the rubber inflation bag of the breathing apparatus and rose swiftly to the surface, where I lifted up in the water and gently dropped back. As I lay there looking upwards, I just remembered to shut off the oxygen valve and remove both the mouthpiece and nose clip. Then, paddling to the side, I climbed out to where the instructor was standing with water dripping from his soaking clothes.

'What did you think you were doing?' he shouted, 'Bloody bell ringing?'

I was saved from any further recriminations by a shout from one of the other trainees in the pool. He had been putting on a show of discovering that he had problems with his ears as soon as they were immersed. In fact, we could all see that he hadn't even started to climb down the ladder properly.

'What do you mean, you can't clear your ears?' came the rejoinder from the unsympathetic chief instructor, 'Bugger me, you ain't even got yourself wet. You must have been down and back up faster than a Tom's draws on a Friday night. You keep going, my son.'

In the end we all seemed to have more or less satisfied him with our progress in simple escape technique, so after a short break he called us together again and we carried on with the tests. By now, we had lost four of our original number through thin eardrums or heavy colds, both of which meant that they couldn't stand the water pressure without pain.

It was time to really find out if the rest of us would be affected by the still higher pressures we could possibly encounter at far greater depths. For this they used a compression chamber. Accompanied with an instructor, four of us at a time filed into the large, steel drum-shaped vessel and took our places on stools placed around its sides. Once the door had been closed, we heard the sound of pumps starting up as air was forced under pressure into the chamber.

'This is where we really test your ears,' the instructor had told us encouragingly. 'The pressure is going to be increased to the equivalent of about 100ft of water. If you can't clear your ears and they begin to hurt, tell me immediately and we'll stop increasing the pressure. Don't panic though,' he added happily, 'even if the worst happens and your ear drums do perforate, the pain would stop immediately. It could leave you a bit deaf for a while, but it will heal up in about a month and be as good as new again! And by the way, don't worry about getting the bends, 'cos we won't be at pressure for long enough.' I learned later that piercing your ears with a needle or something similarly sharp was a somewhat painful way of getting out of having to serve in submarines. At the time submarine duty wasn't entirely voluntary and there were quite a few people who didn't want to spend their service down amongst the fishes.

The pressure started to increase, and by the time it was equivalent to a depth of 60ft or so of water, we had to continually close off our noses with thumb and forefinger and snort to clear our ears. Once we had passed the 60ft level it seemed to even off and thankfully we discovered that we didn't need do it so often. We lost two more trainees at 30ft and another with ear pains at 60ft.

By the time we had reached a pressure equivalent to 100ft of water, the air inside the chamber was more than three times that of normal atmospheric conditions and it had become pretty warm. We were all perspiring freely. The pressure was held constant for a few minutes and then released. As the air expanded once again, the temperature quickly dropped. Soon we were shivering instead, and the condensing water droplets formed into a thin fog, filling the chamber. We clambered out, to be informed that the preliminary tests were now complete. Gratefully, we changed back into our uniforms and wandered back to our mess, tired but probably more than a little elated.

Next day we turned up again at the escape tank to carry on with the training schedule, though by now we were somewhat reduced in numbers. After changing into trunks again we took the lift up ten floors to the big, brightly lit room at the very top of the tower. In the middle, projecting about 3ft above floor level, was the top of the huge, cylindrical tank of water, a wooden rail running around its rim. By standing at its edge, we could look over the rail and down through clear, bluey-green water to the bottom, 100ft below. The depth of water in the tank was equivalent to the height of a ten-storey building and was marked off at every 10ft with a series of black circles painted on the inside wall. A number of hatches and portholes were visible in the sides of the tank to about halfway down, whilst a series of lamps hung in the water on cables, clearly illuminating the tank right to the bottom. All the windows in the large room where we were gathered had been blacked out, but the whole area around the pool was lit by more arc lights located up in the roof.

A naval officer sat in a chair on a small platform suspended over the edge of the pool. Below him, floating on the surface of the water was a large viewer, which provided him with a clear view of everything below. He was surrounded by a bank of controls, connected to a small crane hanging over the water as well as a series of loudspeakers and microphones set into the sides of the tank. Using these, he could not only see everything that was happening far below, but he could also give out instructions, his voice carrying easily through the water from the loudspeakers.

In one corner, looking a bit like a large boiler, we spied a decompression chamber; for trainees who had problems with their lungs or ear drums, I guessed. Anyone suffering from the 'bends' could be placed inside the chamber and the pressure slowly reduced from the equivalent of 100ft of water to that of normal atmosphere. That way, it let the gasses escape from their blood at a carefully regulated rate and didn't create bubbles in their blood.

We were told that first we would be given a buoyancy test.

'This is just a simple test to see whether you are negatively or positively buoyant,' the instructor explained to us. 'In other words to find out whether you normally sink or float in water.'

So we collected our nose clips and goggles from the racks at the side of the room and climbed down the short ladders bolted to the sides of the tank and into the warmish water of the pool.

'OK,' the instructor continued, 'just let go of the ladders, put your hands to your sides and let yourself go. You'll go under at first and then you should come back slowly to the surface. Don't worry,' he added, 'if you don't come up, I'll come down for you and fetch you up.'

With these encouraging words still ringing in my ears, I did as he said and sank beneath the surface. To my relief I found that I slowly rose upwards again. My head broke the surface and I found that I could lie back on the water, relaxed and quite still, hands held at my sides, without sinking. After a minute or two of floating like this, the instructor seemed satisfied and nodded for me to come out. I swam over to the side and clutched at the ladder again.

1 Training aircraft carrier HMS *Theseus*. (Reproduced by kind permission of the National Museum of the Royal Navy)

2 HM Queen Elizabeth and HRH Prince Philip being 'piped' ashore after taking a sail past salute by the Home Fleet.

3 Royal Yacht HMS *Britannia*.

4 'P' boat 'attacking' HMS *Theseus* at 40 knots off the south coast, July 1956.

5 *Right:* 'P' boats coming up fast astern and passing HMS *Ocean,* July 1956.

6 *Below:* Refuelling at sea.

7 *Top:* Carlsberg Brewery, Copenhagen.

8 *Above:* Entrance to Carlsberg Brewery, Copenhagen.

9 *Left:* Helsinki War Memorial.

10 *Above:* The
Submarine Escape
Training Tank
decompression
chamber; always
on hand for any
emergencies.

11 *Right:* A training
session in progress
at the SETT.
(Reproduced by kind
permission of the
SETT administrators)

12 *Above:* Submarine HMS *Sturdy*. (Reproduced by kind permission of the National Museum of the Royal Navy)

13 *Left:* The rock of Gibraltar.

14 *Below:* A unique photograph of HMS *Hood, Rodney, Sussex, Southampton, Sheffield, Aurora* and *Galatea*, all gathered together in Gibraltar harbour at the outset of the Second World War, more than a decade before the visit of HMS *Sturdy* described in this book. (Reproduced by kind permission of the National Museum of the Royal Navy)

15 *Right:* A welcoming smile from a Gibraltar Barbary ape resident. (Reproduced by kind permission of the Gibraltar Tourist Board)

16 *Below:* Submarine depot ship HMS *Maidstone*. (Reproduced by kind permission of the National Museum of the Royal Navy)

17 HMS *Victory*. (Reproduced by kind permission of the National Museum of the Royal Navy)

18 Plaque indicating where Admiral Nelson fell on the deck of HMS *Victory*. (Reproduced by kind permission of the National Museum of the Royal Navy)

'Right,' I heard him say. 'That confirms you're positively buoyant. As it happens, most people are, but we've got to check first, just to make sure. We dredge the bottom of the tank daily,' he added jokingly, 'to find any of you that weren't.'

Next, two of us climbed into a sort of diving bell, with a round, steel floor, open sides and a domed roof. It was slung over the surface of the pool suspended from the jib of the crane I had seen and controlled from the officer's console. With a rush which made our ears pop, we were dropped down through the water until we could see the figure of 20ft alongside on the wall of the tank.

Standing up inside the bell, I discovered that my head and shoulders remained out of the water, and I could breathe easily enough in the air pocket trapped under the domed roof. I took a deep breath, as instructed before we had descended, ducked under the opening in the side of the steel bell and stepped out, keeping my hands at my sides. Then, putting my head back, I started to float upwards to the surface above, blowing out a slow, steady stream of bubbles. I rose up through the silent, bluey-green water and followed the stream of air bubbles upwards towards the mirror-like surface, checking-off the depth markings on the side of the tank.

The air in my lungs had been breathed in at a pressure equivalent to about 20ft of water, the pressure inside the diving bell. So breathing out slowly helped to equalise the pressure inside my lungs with that out-side my body as I rose. By the time I reached the surface I should have adjusted again to the normal atmospheric pressure of the air in the room above. On the way up, I began to think I was blowing out too fast, but as my head broke the surface into fresh air again, I found to my relief that the air left in my lungs had expanded, and I could breathe normally again. I swam to the side of the tank, mounted the ladder and thankfully climbed out of the pool.

Two more ascents followed, this time from depths of 30 and then 60ft, but without using a diving bell. Set into the side of the tank were a series of escape compartments which could be entered from outside. After closing the bulkheads, a stop cock was opened and water allowed to flood the chamber until the pressures inside equalled that of the water outside. The hatch connecting it to the tank could then be opened. As the hatch reached only halfway up the chamber, the water level rose above the opening until the pressures equalised inside and out and a large bubble of air under pressure was held at the roof of the chamber for us to stand up in and breathe. We could then take a deep breath, duck down to stoop under the hatch exit and leave the airlock into the main body of water in the tank.

After that it was a repeat of the diving bell and by the time we were down to the 60ft level, I was beginning to enjoy myself. The water was pleasantly clear and warm, as we made a silent ascent with a steady stream of bubbles rising upwards towards the mirrored surface. Bands of black depth markers slowly passed by, and seemed to create a surreal effect in the greenish light.

After a break, the time came to test out what they said would be as near to the 'real thing' as they could make it. Not an escape from a damaged submarine under actual disaster conditions, but from a mock-up of a submarine compartment built into the base of the 100ft tower of water.

We went down to the ground-floor level again in the lift and trooped through a watertight door into the simulated control room of a submerged submarine. There in the centre was the usual steel ladder, leading up to a watertight hatch in the roof above. Normally this would lead up to the inside of a conning tower but this one was set into the floor of the water tank above. It was held tightly shut by the pressure of water outside. Hanging down from a collar surrounding the hatch to about 4ft from the deck was a canvas chute – or twill trunk, as it was called – held taut by a number of guy ropes tied to floor shackles. The ladder disappeared up inside this chute to the hatch above. The instructor shut the door behind us and, as he fastened its securing bolts, we crowded around in a nervous circle inside the dimly lit compartment, the floor still wet from an earlier test.

'This'll be your final ascent,' he said, 'and this time you'll be going up the full depth of the tank. To make it a bit more realistic, we've made it look like a real submarine's control room. The actual ascent won't be any harder than before – in fact most people say it's easier. But before I flood the compartment, I'd better explain exactly what we'll be doing. This time, you'll be using the BIBS breathing gear, just to get used to it. You don't actually need it to do the escape test, but submarines are now fitted with them, so it's just as well to get used to them.'

We donned the rubberised immersion suits, which had sealing bands at the wrists and ankles. The double rubber layer could be inflated between its layers to give extra buoyancy – a useful aid for anyone who didn't float naturally. Attached at the thighs were inflatable gloves, a whistle and a sea water lamp; all needed for any long-term survival in rough, cold seas.

'These tubes,' the petty officer indicated a number of rubber tubes ending in mouthpieces which hung down from a pipeline in the ceiling, 'are attached to oxygen bottles. They're not pure oxygen as that would cause oxygen poisoning, but when I turn on this valve, you can each take a mouthpiece and start breathing into them. As you breathe out, a valve opens in the line, so that you don't breathe in the same air again.'

He turned a stop-cock and took a mouthpiece himself to demonstrate. 'And to make it a bit more realistic, we'll turn off all the lights and just use the torches, which are always kept handy.' As he spoke, he switched on a torch and swung the light around the gloomy compartment to check that we were all breathing through mouthpieces.

We huddled in a semi-circle around him, the semi-darkness now lit only by the two or three available torches. Satisfied that all was as it should be, he started to open up the compartment flood valves. Almost immediately, water came pouring from several holes in the floor. As it rose inside the small space, the air pressure began to increase – and so too did the temperature. Soon we were all sweating in the humid conditions and we began to clear the pressure before it could build up in our ears.

The water had soon risen to about chest height. Then it stopped. The bottom opening of the twill tube was now a couple of feet below the water's surface and opening an air vent inside the tube had allowed the level to rise inside until it was filled with a column of water as well. By then, the pressure of the air left for us to breathe in the top few feet of the compartment was equal to that in the water of the tank above. We were ready to try out the escape drill and as I was standing nearest to the ladder, it seemed that I would get the honour of going first.

The suits were partly inflated by connecting them briefly to the outlet valve on the BIBS near the mouthpiece, allowing exhaled air to fill the space between inside and outside layers. I put a nose clip on, adjusted my goggles and took a deep breath. As I gripped the bottom edge of the twill trunk under water, I let the mouthpiece drop from my mouth, ducked under the water's surface and started to climb up the ladder inside to the hatch, holding my breath. Quickly I slipped off the clips and climbed out into the tank.

Immediately I was held by two instructors, who had been waiting in the diving bell nearby. When they were satisfied that I had put my head back and started to blow out a steady trickle of bubbles, they let me go and I started to rise. I found out later that anyone who forgot to breathe out got a sharp punch in the chest to ensure that they did.

Since I was wearing an inflated suit this time, I rose much more quickly towards the water's surface, – but there was much further to go! Or at least that was the impression I got as I shot up in a flurry of bubbles, swinging about wildly as I rose. The marked-off depths on the side of the pool seemed to shoot past – 80, 70, 60 – by the time the 50ft mark appeared, I was sure that I had breathed out too quickly and I wouldn't have enough air left. But then as I reached the 30 and 20 marks, I found that the air in my lungs had kept on expanding and I could still breathe out.

I looked upwards, and the bright, mirrored surface seemed to rush towards me. I broke the surface and my impetus lifted me partly out of the water. I fell onto my back gasping, and lay there for a minute or two while I recovered my breath. Then, feeling elated, I paddled to the side and climbed out. I started to feel like a real submariner.

My reverie was short-lived. Behind me the pool's surface erupted and a figure lifted up, coughing and spluttering. 'Cor,' the figure gasped, 'I thought I'd 'ad it there for a moment.'

The rubber-suited figure proved to be that of Jonesy, who recovered enough after a while to clamber out of the pool.

'I 'ad a bloody coughing fit 'alfway up and nearly drowned mun,' he gasped, hanging on to the side of the pool and coughing up what seemed like half the tank-full of water.

One by one the rest of the group resurfaced and after exchanging experiences, we went back down in the lift to change back into our uniforms. The instructor came in as we were finishing and told us that we had all passed the tests.

Later that afternoon we transferred to the nearby base at HMS *Dolphin* for final submarine training. The next morning we were issued with new HMS *Dolphin* hatbands. I began to feel that perhaps now I was more than just an ordinary national serviceman. Things were looking up; perhaps it wasn't going to be so bad after all!

Chapter 9

Never Volunteer

HMS *Dolphin* was situated in the old fort blockhouse, a stone's throw away from where we had spent the last couple of days. The big, squat, stone fortress was originally completed in the early eighteenth century, then added to regularly ever since and taken over by the navy early in the twentieth century. It was built on a spit of land that formed one side of Portsmouth harbour. Hence it was surrounded on the other three sides by water; Haslar Creek on one side, Portsmouth harbour mouth and the open sea on the other two. It dominated the narrow stretch of water opposite the town itself and commanded a view of all approaching ships. There was a small, stony beach and jetty on the sheltered, creek side, with a tidy row of carefully whitewashed stones bordering steps that led into the base. Nearby, out of the water and up on wooden blocks, stood a veteran T-class submarine; no longer in commission and just there as a reminder of a previous decade.

The main entrance into the base was further round on the narrow landward side, at a break in the wide, turreted wall that surrounded the imposing fort. Here, a smartly uniformed sentry stood all day just inside the gates, checking on any visitors. Inside were a jumble of offices and barracks housed either within the fort's old stone battlements and storehouses or in a number of more recent wooden huts. The Flag Officer of Submarines (the FOSM) was based here and the navy had added a jumble of accommodation blocks and workshops on both the inside and outside of the huge stone battlements.

I soon discovered that HMS *Dolphin* had a number of unique features. Not only was it the oldest fortress in the country still used by the military, but it also had accommodation blocks named after long-defunct ships and a canteen situated in an old Nissen tin hut. This latter was located conveniently next door to the sick bay and the patients were often to be seen in the canteen supping what they insisted were medicinal liquids. The submarine base could also boast a post office which unofficially doubled up as one of the first betting shops in Gosport!

Most of the navy personnel at the base were there for training, or else they were in transit between commissions. Apart from the permanent administration staff, most people were either waiting to join a boat or they were on leave following a completed tour of duty. I soon discovered that most people there thought of it as a pretty 'cushy' billet since by comparison with that of the average submarine, accommodation at HMS *Dolphin* was like a five-star hotel. There was also the added bonus of being able to get into Gosport or Portsmouth on evenings off – for anyone who hadn't already spent all their money of course!

During our stay at *Dolphin*, we went through an intensive course in operating and repairing the whole range of submarine machinery. This meant that we had to learn about everything that moved or turned around. In the training school we tried out just about all the machines that kept the submarine going, from the enormous sixteen-cylinder diesel engines (two of which seemed to be the main source of propulsion on many of the boats), to the pumps, generators, refrigerators and their associated controls. The sound of a diesel engine at half speed seemed loud enough to make any speech nearby pointless, so I couldn't imagine what two engines running together at full throttle in the confined space of a submarine's engine room must sound like. I found out soon enough.

Apart from the normal chores and lectures that were part of our training, the only downside seemed to be that we had to take it in turns to do guard duty. Usually this was at night time on a four-hour shift. It was probably all right in the summertime, but this was February and not only dark but cold as well. It meant that we had to leave the warm comfort of our mess to spend four hours or so around the dark and mostly silent instruction rooms and barracks, but particularly along the perimeter wall.

The ancient fort walls were wide enough for a path to run around near the top and about 3 or 4ft below the outside face. In a castle they would probably be called the ramparts. From up there you could look down the walls to the sea below and see if anyone was foolish enough to try and get in. At about this time – the late 1950s – the IRA had been particularly active and they had been causing trouble on the mainland as well as their heartlands in Northern Ireland. The military establishments, including those of the navy, were getting edgy and security had been tightened.

The Admiralty may have considered guard duty a necessity under the circumstances, but on a cold and windy night in February it wasn't very popular with those of us who had to do it. Occasionally there was snow or sleet to contend with as well as the howling wind, so we tended to search out the nooks and crannies where you could shelter for a while and have an undisturbed smoke. Unfortunately the officers and petty officers in charge also knew that the appointed guards couldn't always be relied on to stay awake or be alert all the time. So they carried out spot checks at different times during the night. They would quietly approach any unsuspecting guard to see if he was sufficiently awake to challenge them – and of course, whether he did it in the correct manner as set out in Admiralty regulations.

Probably we didn't take the job seriously enough. But the navy did, and to emphasise the fact, they even issued the relevant guards with a rifle. Not exactly a modern weapon; it was, in fact, an old Lee and Enfield that probably hadn't been fired for the last twenty years. And just to make sure that there weren't any accidents, they didn't supply any bullets with the gun. So the guards had to patrol the perimeter of the fort carrying a rifle which didn't come with any bullets. Nobody really explained to us what you were supposed to do if you actually found an intruder. Hitting them over the head with the rifle didn't seem like a good idea and it would probably have been a rather drastic thing to do anyway – particularly if the person attacked was completely blameless. Nonetheless we were instructed to be sure to challenge the officer carrying out the rounds as he would be checking up on us.

That particular night it was my turn to take the least popular middle watch from one minute past midnight to four in the morning. I duly collected and signed for the greatcoat, belt and heavy, antiquated rifle at the gatehouse. Then I made my way out into the night and eventually found Bill, who I was due to relieve, sheltering behind one of the offices near the cook house. Having gone through the standard rigmarole for taking over duty from him, I made a circuit of the perimeter and started my four-hour lonely stint by first of all sheltering in a corner of the store area for a forbidden smoke.

Over the next couple of dreary hours, I carried out a desultory check as required; along the sea walls and around the mess buildings and maze of offices scattered around the base. All the while I was trying to keep awake and desperately trying to keep warm in the freezing night air. Roll on four o'clock I thought! There were a number of shielded lights dotted around the base, but most of the area was dark, silent and cold. Wandering along the path on top of the sea wall and leaning over the ramparts, I could easily make out the bright lights of Portsmouth just across the water.

At this spot on the perimeter wall, the Blockhouse Fort fronted on to the harbour mouth, where the stretch of sea was little more than a hundred yards wide. Though it was dark all around, I could just make out by the light from the houses and pubs on the far side that the tide was on the turn. It was moving at a fair pace, since all the water in the harbour had to force its way through the narrow entrance before the next tide. From the noisy singing and laughter carrying across from the pub opposite, I reckoned that they must be a lot warmer and having a far better evening than I was. And it was officially after drinking hours too! Perhaps it was a party.

Theoretically the checks by the duty officer were supposed to be random, but we all knew that they weren't any happier to be out on nights like this than we were. So you could be fairly sure that they would get it over with early on in the watch, and that was when you had to keep alert and make sure you kept an eye open for any movement.

Sure enough, before the watch was halfway through, I spied a couple of figures approaching me along a path near the officers' mess. It was the master-at-arms, accompanied by the duty officer. They were lighting their way with a torch and I waited for them to get well within earshot and in clear view. When they were near enough, I gave the time-honoured challenge of 'Who goes there, friend or foe?' I waited for the usual reply of 'friend', before calling out for them to 'Advance and be recognised.' To my dismay I heard the reply 'foe' instead.

The manual didn't seem to cover this situation. I was rather lost for what to do next, so in the end I decided to try again – using a different approach. 'I'll have to take you in custody to the guardhouse,' I finally told them.

'You've got no bullets in that gun,' said the officer, 'how are you going to manage that?'

That had me in a quandary for a minute, but it was cold and I was tired, which probably explains why it gave me the courage to answer back. I was in no mood for officers playing 'silly beggars'.

'If you were a real enemy, you wouldn't bloody well know that, would you?' I answered sharply. 'And as it happens I recognise you as the duty officer, Lieutenant Commander Atkins. I've seen you around the base.'

That took him aback a bit and though it was rather grudgingly, it seemed to satisfy him. With the master-at-arms present as a witness, he couldn't very well do much else. They went on their way, and the rest of that night passed without further incident. Luckily, I didn't meet him again on guard duty to find out if he bore me any grudges.

Perhaps it was just a coincidence, or maybe it was the same awkward sod that I heard about when I was out in Malta a few months later. When I was in Valletta, a stoker from one of the ships anchored out in the harbour told me about an encounter he had had with an officer only a few days previously. It seems he was on duty in the ship's motor launch, ferrying crews back and forward to the shore, when on one of his trips he had picked up this slightly worse for wear lieutenant commander returning from a party ashore. He related the story:

'"You boy," the officer had said, slightly slurring his words. They had gone about halfway out to the ship. "Do you do everything your commanding officer tells you – without question?"

"Er – yes sir," I answered, a bit suspiciously. 'Cause I had heard that he could be an awkward bugger, he told me.

"Well then," he says, "throw me overboard – and that's an order."

Ee's up to his tricks again, I thinks. Testing me to see if I gets scared. So I doesn't move.

"Do you hear me?" he shouts. "Throw me overboard."

You don't fool me, I thinks, and I just grins. Worst thing I could 'ave done, as it turns out.

"If you don't throw me overboard," he says, "I'm going to throw you overboard. Now, for the last time, throw me overboard, at once."

He's on his feet by now, jumping about. And I don't like the look of things very much. Still, you can't chuck an officer in the Oggin, can you, so I don't do nothing. Still, he can't throw me in neither, I thinks. That's where I was wrong – and he made me swim back to the ship too!'" he told me miserably. 'The bastard knew I wouldn't dare put in a complaint.'

Whether it was the same officer that I had met on guard duty or not, I never discovered.

Apart from some memorable visits ashore in Gosport and Portsmouth, my time in HMS *Dolphin* otherwise seemed to pass uneventfully. I had been there for about a month when I got the chance to play for the base against another naval team also based in Portsmouth. It must have been because I had mentioned that I had played a bit of football back home for a local team rather than any obvious talent I showed for the game.

The opposing team's ground was a few miles away near Southsea and we all travelled there in a smart new Admiralty coach. The game was going pretty well and about halfway through the second half, with our team two goals in the lead, Smithy crossed the ball over to the wing where I was playing. Before I could gather it in properly, the opposing fullback came at me in a vicious sliding tackle, obviously determined to stop any further humiliation for their team. As I went down hard, I managed to twist my knee and felt it give way under me. I lay there in pain for a while, trying to recover and get back on my feet. The game was temporarily halted while a few of our team gathered around with sympathetic enquiries and offering to 'duff up' the rival player.

Eventually however, after some tentative hobbling around, I had to be helped off the pitch. By then, any suggestion of a fight had been forgotten. The match ended with *Dolphin* being victorious, but I ended up in the naval hospital at Haslar and I spent the next month with a suspected torn hamstring. I underwent a week of painful testing, but the doctors finally decided it wasn't going to break after all and I ought to rest the leg instead. So apart from undergoing deep heat treatment and flirting with one or two of the nurses, I didn't do very much for the next few weeks. It didn't help very much that I couldn't even go into Pompey for the night. It was during this spell of enforced inactivity that I got chatting with the occupant of the bed next to mine and he told me with some pride how he came to be there.

Hughie came from Glasgow. He was a tall, well-built Scotsman, who had got married before his seventeenth birthday. Two years later he already had a 'couple of bairns' – as he put it. He was a fighter – and had the broken nose to prove it. It was as a result of one of his regular bouts that he was in Haslar at the time. Usually he came out victorious from most of his skirmishes, but apparently last time someone had managed to get to him first with a bottle.

I heard later that he went on to box for the camp, though he was a brawler really, not a boxer. He just pummelled his opponents into submission – usually winning his matches with a knockout. Any damage he sustained in the ring was never as bad as the knocks and bruises or often worse that apparently he had suffered earlier in the back alleys of the Gorbals back home. I noticed that although he got on fairly well with most of his fellow trainees and was generally accepted in the ward where we were, he would occasionally show the cruel streak that had helped him to survive up till now. At such times he was given a wide birth by some: 'It canna be hurtin' ye,' he would say as he gave some victim's arm a vicious twist, 'I canna feel a thing'.

The last job he had had before joining the navy was as a coal miner and on one occasion he recounted some of his experiences in the job to us:

'I mind one day last summer,' he recalled, 'I was due to work the afternoon shift, yee ken, and the heat was so bad that the sweat was runnin' off us. We didna feel like workin' in yon heat, but we couldna think of any excuse. Well young Jamie Robertson takes a walk int' canteen an' picks up a jam sandwich. He opens it up and there's a wee thin smear of jam in it. "Hey," he says "I wan' more jam than this for ma two pennies." "Sorry," says the girl, "ye canna have any more, there is'na any." "Right," says Jamie, "get your things lads, we're commin' oot." And we stay'd oot on strike 'till the weather broke a few days later.'

'Och, it's quite true,' he went on, as there were hoots of disbelief from the others in the ward who had gathered around. 'Miners get a good wage yee ken, and we could easily afford a few days off now and again, 'specially if they thought it was an accident. Then we got paid for not working as well.'

He thought for a moment as if considering whether to divulge a secret and then, obviously deciding it was safe with us, he carried on in a confidential tone.

'I mind the time when a mate of mine put a long crowbar through the grill of the cage. You ken, the lift we use to come up to the surface in. Well, it was long enough to stick out through each side see. Yon cage driver was in on it as well, see, so he put it into full speed and of course the crowbar caught up on the sides of the shaft. It ripped the doors off and damaged the floor of the cage as well. We took out the crowbar and dropped it down the shaft so they would think it was an accident. We was off for three days on full pay while they repaired the damage,' he added wistfully. 'Then the weather broke, so we's all went back to work.'

On balance, I was rather glad that he wasn't on any of the submarines with me. Otherwise, I might have been trying out the escape routines sooner than expected.

CHAPTER 10

WELCOME TO BELFAST

It was only after a few more weeks spent recuperating in Haslar that the doctors eventually decided I was well enough to resume duties and I was immediately given a transfer to HMS *Maidstone*, the submarine depot ship. On arrival, I discovered that it was not only used in its originally intended role as a support vessel but it also took part in goodwill tours and for general training purposes. Years later, after the navy had finished with it, I heard that it had been converted into a prison ship; but right now it was due to sail for Belfast.

The *Maidstone* was based down at Portland in Dorset. This time I didn't have to go on the train to take up my posting, but instead got a lift by naval transport. Early one morning I slung my kit in the back of the covered lorry and bounced all the way to where the *Maidstone* was anchored. I made my way through the dockyard and as I clambered up the gangplank I saw that the bulk of Portland Bill was plainly visible in the background.

Not even its makers on Clydebank could call the *Maidstone* a beautiful ship and by now it was also beginning to show its age. It had definitely seen better days! Probably 'functional' would have described it better now. Built several years before the Second World War, the *Maidstone* had seen service all over the world – but particularly in the Mediterranean and the Pacific.

Not only could it support a fleet of submarines, with all its necessary supplies of food, fuel, spares and torpedoes etc., it also had facilities to charge their batteries and carry out their repairs for them. In fact, if necessary it could provide a squadron of submarines with everything they needed, without them having to come into port at all.

The *Maidstone* was equipped with a foundry, several machinery shops, plumbing and electrical shops, as well as an operating theatre, a hospital and a dental surgery complete with qualified medical staff. There were canteens, a laundry, chapel, bakery, cinema and even a barber's shop. Crammed within its 500ft length of rusting steel hull was a whole floating city. It took me most of the journey to Northern Ireland to even get my bearings and confidently find my way around the bewildering maze of decks and corridors.

I was assigned to help out in the foundry – a large, dusty workshop way down in the bowels of the ship. There I sweated away in the heat from the furnace, alongside a burly, affable, middle-aged chief petty officer named CPO Stevens who was in charge. Before starting his long career in the navy, he had learned his trade as an apprentice in a Tyneside steel works. Soon after I met him, I learned that he only had three more years to run before his retirement.

There wasn't much that CPO Stevens didn't know about casting. He wasn't just a craftsman, but an artist in his work. Most of the work in the foundry was for one-off repairs and the methods used were the same type of sand casting that had been used for thousands of years. It was in the days before die-casting, investment casting and other mass production techniques took over.

The *Maidstone* set off into the English Channel but soon after we had weighed anchor, I learned that we had to cast a phosphor-bronze propeller at sea. It had to be ready for replacing a damaged one when we arrived in Belfast. By that time, the winds had increased in force and even in a ship the size of *Maidstone* we felt its effects. By the time we had started to get the furnace going and sorted out the moulds there was a distinct pitching and rolling, even in the foundry well down below the main deck. The CPO's skills were soon to be tested to the full.

First we placed the wooden propeller moulding in the bottom of a casting box, better known as a drag, which had a separate steel bottom plate. The wooden moulding was then packed around with a special mix of lake sand and clay, leaving half of the wooden mould protruding above the flattened top surface of the sand mix, which we had left level with the top of the drag box sides. Then the top, open half of the casting box (or the cope), was placed on its locating pegs, more sand mix packed in until the level was at the top of the cope, and the lid finally located and fixed down.

We could now turn the casting boxes over, carefully lifting off the drag and even more carefully removing the propeller mould. It was then that the years of expertise really showed. The 'chief' delicately smoothed and corrected any faults or voids left behind and added 'parting' sand to give a fine, smooth finish to the surface. A fixing compound was painted on, and 'gates' or pouring holes pierced through the top layer of sand, as well as a series of risers to let out steam or gas when the metal was poured in. Finally the cope half of the casting box was gingerly lifted back on to its locating pegs whilst we waited for the furnace to heat up. Soon it had reached melting temperature and was hot enough for all the metal ingots inside to have melted.

Using a crucible on a long, two-handled cradle, we filled it with liquid metal from the furnace and poured the white hot, molten fluid slowly and very carefully down the gates into the casting box, all the while trying to avoid any bubbles forming. We also had to try and stay upright against the pitching and rolling motion of the ship, desperately trying to avoid missing the pouring holes altogether and tipping the molten liquid on our feet instead. By the time we had finished, I was perspiring profusely – and not just from the heat of the furnace. Since it was to be several more hours before we could examine the fruits of our labours it was then a case of just waiting.

The cooling period was one of the most critical phases of the oper-ation. We had to set up a number of heaters around the casting box to cool it slowly and help to make sure that the casting cooled evenly throughout. We had time to go back to the mess and eat, as we waited impatiently to find out if the casting was not only strong enough, but also stress-free and without voids. We had almost reached Belfast by the time the chief decided it would probably be safe to break open the casting box and examine the fruits of our work.

The metal had cooled sufficiently for us to clear away all the sand and cut off any excess metal that had run into the riser vents. It still looked a little rough to me, but after a brief examination, and using a hammer to test for the resonance effects, the chief pronounced his satisfaction with the finished product. Finished that was, as far as we were concerned, but before it could be fitted to the awaiting submarine, it still had to be sent off for machining and buffing in order to reduce the drag and resistance of sea water. This was practically the most important part of the exercise, since it had to be finished to a glass-like surface. It would help to cut down noise, and hence the chances of being detected underwater. It was a job for one of the highly skilled machine shops located elsewhere in the bowels of the ship.

In the end, I never got to see the finished propeller. Nor did I see it being fitted to the waiting boat. But I was still left with a satisfying sense of achievement, even, perhaps, of having done something useful. It was probably the first time that I had felt anything like that either in or out of the services.

We tied up in Victoria channel, opposite Queen's Island and the Harland and Wolff shipyard. We were only going to be there for a few days. Our main reason for being there at all was to supply the crippled submarine with its new propeller, together with any other repairs or supplies it needed.

It was a further couple of days before we could go ashore. In fact not until the feverish activity aboard ship had begun to die down. It was evening time and there was a light sprinkling of rain coming down from the darkening skies. It wasn't a very inviting prospect, but as we had never been to Belfast before and in spite of the duty officer's warnings, four of us had decided it warranted a visit.

'Keep out of trouble,' we had been instructed, 'don't get into any dis-cussions about religion; don't go near the Falls Road area; and whatever you do, if you go into any pubs don't order a Black and Tan.' The first bit we all understood, but as to the rest of it, we were a bit bemused. We had heard that there was some sort of tension in Belfast, and we knew all about the Orange Day marches and riots on the so called 'Glorious Twelfth', but it was a few years before all 'the Troubles' and the IRA hadn't started to become everyday news. At the time, in our ignorance, we knew very little about any of it.

We set out and made our way past the silent cranes and buildings towards the dock gates that led out onto Corporation Street. Just inside the dock gates stood a guard hut with its outside lamp casting a pool of light across the road. There were two men inside the lighted room and we went over to ask directions. To our surprise they seemed reticent to answer our que-ries. Finally, having decided that we didn't pose any kind of a threat, one of them grudgingly came to the door. To our surprise, he first switched off the outer light, together with the central light inside the room.

Even more surprisingly, he asked us to move into the shadows at the side of the hut. Only then did he seem to relax a bit and gave us directions to the town centre. When we asked if the Falls Road was anywhere near there, his suspicious attitude seemed to return again. He too suggested that we should give the area a miss, and it was only when we jokingly remarked on the strange ritual of turning off the lights that the watchman seemed to realise our obvious innocence.

'To be sure,' he explained, 'I'm not in a hurry to get meself shot at, am I?'

It transpired that only a month earlier, a colleague had been shot and seriously wounded as he stood silhouetted against the light in front of the hut. I don't think any of us really believed him – this was 1957 after all and we were in the UK, not in some so-called banana republic!

A few years later, of course, when we all started to hear about the atrocities carried out in Belfast, we probably began to appreciate a little of what it meant to live in constant fear of the IRA. By that time, Bernadette Devlin, Martin McGuiness, Ian Paisley and Gerry Adams had become household names. But on that cold and wet winter's evening we didn't concern ourselves with the RUC, the Apprentice Boys or even about 'Bloody Sunday'. Instead, we carried on along North Street towards the Shankhill Road and Falls Street areas.

We began to notice that a lot of the buildings were scruffy-looking and that most of the shops were protected by steel shutters. The walls were covered in graffiti and crude wall drawings of paramilitary figures bearing guns. There were several 'Kill the Pope' slogans and 'F★★★ the Proddies'. You could almost taste the hate in the air. There were very few people about, and nowhere seemed to be open.

It was still only nine o'clock in the evening; early for us. We passed a burnt-out building and then saw the lights of a pub ahead which appeared to be open. On entering, we noticed that there were several small groups of men sitting huddled in quiet conversation at the tables. They looked up suspiciously as we walked in.

It was probably out of a sense of bravado or bloody mindedness that we all decided to order a Black and Tan; a mixture of pale ale and stout. During our briefing on the ship we had been warned that it evoked catholic memories of the hated Royal Irish Constabulary Reserve Force which was eventually disbanded in 1922. But we must have been in a Protestant area, or perhaps it was because there were four of us. For whatever reason, it didn't seem to draw any sort of response, just a sullen demand for payment from the barman that had served us.

Soon afterwards, the door from the street opened and three hard-looking men in their early twenties appeared. Immediately another group who had been sitting talking in low tones near the door got up and left. It didn't look as if we were going to make many new friends that night! By the time we had finished our first round of drinks we all agreed that we had had enough of Belfast. No one looked up as we left the bar. There didn't seem to be much else to do and we made our way back to the docks and found the comfort of our ship. It was the earliest night back that I could remember. Not many of the crew seemed upset either when we left port two days later and set a course for home.

Since there wasn't any urgent, official work to carry out in the foundry on the way back and in fact for the next few days, we were able to resume our other, unofficial tasks. The foundry was often as busy between navy jobs as it was during them, and the production of 'foreigners' took up much of our spare time. We could probably have made a lucrative trade in them, but the cast souvenirs we produced were nearly always favours for the chief's friends or colleagues – and also of course, various officers who got to hear about them.

The most popular item that we made was probably the model of a 'T' class submarine balanced on the upturned tail of a diving dolphin, the shining, polished aluminium alloy pair then mounted on an equally shining, polished wooden base. The two castings were sometimes brazed together permanently and then screwed to the base, but more often they were all demountable for ease of concealment and transport ashore. We couldn't very well send them down to the machine shop for polishing and buffing, so we did it ourselves with the help of files and emery paper. As a finishing touch the whole thing was often fitted with an engraved plaque bearing the person's name or that of the ship. The result was that the models became highly prized amongst fellow submariners.

In the course of my service aboard HMS *Maidstone* I became quite adept at making ashtrays, lamp standards, model ships and a number of other items. This foundry experience and training in new-found skills proved extremely useful in later life. I suppose it all came under the heading of 'alternative skills'. Unfortunately, I didn't ever find a reason to include them in a CV.

CHAPTER 11

SCANDINAVIAN SMORGASBORD

After a short break back at Portland, I learned that the *Maidstone* would be sailing again soon. This time it had been given the task of carrying out a goodwill exercise to Scandinavia. It would involve plenty of pomp and circumstance, with the Royal Marine band and lots of top brass. There were to be official receptions and best uniforms and medals – in fact everything involved with 'showing the flag'. It sounded interesting and would certainly be different from anything up to now! Several other ships would be coming along with us, including a high-profile aircraft carrier and, in order to make the maximum use of what we had, the ships would all be visiting different ports.

Perhaps we drew the short straw, but our first stop was at Kristiansand, on the southern tip of Norway. Most of us had never even heard the name before. It didn't sound much like a big city somehow, with lots of nightlife, but then neither was Portland, which we left in torrential rain a few days later. The rain didn't stop until we had rounded the Kent coast and headed northwards. The weather improved the further we went and by the time we had rendezvoused with the other ships in our group, the sun was shining from a clear blue sky.

Some days later we sailed along the straits of the Skagerrak, passing hundreds of small and mostly uninhabited islands on the way. Then, through a narrow entrance between rocky outcrops, we entered a large, circular, deep-water harbour. All around, pinkish granite rocks glistened in the sunshine, whilst perched on their flat tops and glimpsed through the green pine trees of a forest were hundreds of brightly coloured wooden houses.

By the water's edge stood some simple, wooden docks, at one side of which was a margarine factory and on the other a nickel works. Behind them we caught a glimpse of the town itself, set out in neat rows of shops and offices. Near the centre, surrounded by shady gardens, stood a tall wooden church and opposite was a police station. Later, we discovered that the town's drinking water supply even came from the deep, clear fresh water rock pools in the forest-covered hills at the back of the town. It was all so bright, clean and tidy, that coming after the rather grey, sprawling towns of Scotland and Northern Ireland, it seemed almost like a film set.

We immediately realised that the arrival of the British navy was something of an event and the whole town had turned out to welcome us. The girls all appeared to wear patterned, chunky sweaters, and their short, corn-coloured hair ruffled provocatively in the breeze. It was probably only a fantasy, but compared with the girls of southern Europe, the Norwegian girls gave off the impression of well-curved, healthy figures, bronze skins and widely smiling eyes.

For the next day or so we had plenty of chances to study them in more detail. The ship was thrown open to visitors, the band played topical tunes and the marines put on a display of marching and unarmed combat. For their part, the local inhabitants arranged a show of folk dancing and there were lots of welcoming speeches. That weekend they put on a dance evening. Everywhere there was a festive feeling in the air and although we probably hadn't stayed long enough to get to know the place and people properly, it was with a lot of regret that we sailed away again four days later. Apart from the local onion beer (which was about the only drink in town and then could only be found at a few establishments), our short stay in Kristiansand had proved a huge success. As our ship pulled away from the dockside, it looked as if the whole town had turned out to wave us off. Perhaps we hadn't drawn the short straw after all!

Out in the open seas again, we headed off around the north coast of Denmark towards the Baltic. Somewhere ahead of us was the carrier *Ocean* and, sometimes behind and sometimes alongside, was our escort destroyer. The next destination on the Scandinavian tour was to be Copenhagen – at that time vying with Hamburg for the title of 'Sex city of the north'.

The next morning we were 'attacked' by two of the navy's fast torpedo boats, or 'P' boats as they were called. Without warning, they suddenly appeared astern of us and bore down at enormous speed, having apparently managed to approach within a mile or two without having been noticed. The defending gunners on our ship would have had only a brief moment to find them in the gun sights as they lined up on the ship prior to releasing their torpedoes. Once they had discharged their imaginary weapons, they immediately peeled off to either side of us and disappeared again as fast as they had arrived. During that brief period of lining up to take aim they were extremely vulnerable to an alert and experienced gunner. Torpedo boats presented a small and extremely fast-moving target to aim at, but the life expectancy of a 'P' boat crewman in war-time combat didn't bear thinking about. All they could rely on was their speed, together with the element of surprise, to protect them.

Later we practised the tricky manoeuvre of refuelling at sea. The *Maidstone* was a floating submarine repair and supply ship. It was large, slow and unwieldy and was easy prey to enemy ships. Its best defence was to stay at sea as long as possible, where it could hide in the vast expanse of oceans and only meeting up with its fleet of submarines by secret appointment. So it was a pretty essential tactic to refuel away from port where it would have been easy for an enemy to lie in wait or attack it from the air.

First we had to get the *Maidstone* travelling in a straight line at sufficient speed to overcome any effects from waves and tide etc. Not an easy task at the best of times and even more difficult today because of the sea's swell. Then the refuelling tanker had to draw close alongside and match the *Maidstone*'s direction and speed closely so that there was as little movement between them as possible.

When the two ships were sailing along dangerously close together, a line was fired across to us and the attached filling line swung across on a jib or boom and was attached to our filling nozzle. Then we watched nervously as fuel was pumped across. Then the only thing to do was to trust that the two captains could hold their course and speed for long enough to prevent the pipe being pulled apart, fuel being spilled everywhere and the danger of a fire at sea. It seemed to take ages for the process to be completed, but at last we were all able to breath a sigh of relief as the filling hose was finally detached and swung back before being stowed away safely. The refuelling vessel swung away from us and made off to repeat the process elsewhere, mission completed!

I soon discovered that with goodwill visits there were things that you could, and things that couldn't, do. For instance, you were expected to be in your best uniform much of the time and to be on your best behaviour all of the time. On the other hand, going down to the red light district and getting into any sort of trouble was definitely not encouraged. So calling in to Copenhagen in those days was, for young, red-blooded males like us, a bit like being taken along to a sweet shop and then being told you mustn't sample the goodies. So, with that thought much in mind, the first thing we did when the last visitor had departed and we finally got some shore leave was to act like a tourist and visit Copenhagen's number one attraction, the Little Mermaid. We reckoned the Admiralty would have approved of that.

It turned out that the small, rather lonely looking naked statue, sitting on its half legs, half tail, alone on a rock by the water's edge wasn't, in fact, very far away from where we were docked. Not surprisingly, the shine was long gone from its smooth surface, since it had apparently already been there for over fifty years. Any shine was now largely replaced by greenish verdigris.

'Hey, look at this,' called Phil, who had been reading all about it on a plaque nearby. 'It says here that the Little Mermaid was donated to the city by the founder of the Carlsberg Brewery.'

Naturally, when we read that the benefactor was an original member of the Carlsberg family, we all decided straight away that we ought to pay a visit to his brewery. Phil had read in his guidebook that they provided samples of their products to any visitors and this may also have influenced the decision a bit.

The brewery, together with its visitors' reception hall, was on the other side of Copenhagen and past the popular Tivoli Gardens. Getting there took us past the central station, which interestingly also led us into the red light area around Istedgade. By that time, it was the middle of the afternoon and there wasn't much to see – apart from streets full of sex shops. We spent some time studying what, at that time, would have been considered illicit magazines and contraptions; although by present-day standards they would probably be considered 'old hat'. Sometime later we made our way into the Tivoli Gardens themselves and concentrated on some of the more conventional pleasures. For the next couple of hours we hurtled around the old wooden rollercoaster, took a boat ride on the dragon lake, stood before the huge, rotating carousel, walked around the Pantomime Theatre, the glass hall and the fairytale castle. Finally we collapsed into chairs in one of the open-air cafés for a reviving drink – a

Carlsberg, of course! Years afterwards, Disneyland had copied the Tivoli formula with equal success, but they couldn't match that drink.

Recovered somewhat, we exited from the Tivoli, and having first of all taken a few wrong turnings, we discovered that the Carlsberg Brewery was, in fact, not very far from the gardens we had just left. At the visitors' reception we found out that they held regular, organised tours – complete with English-speaking guide, and we latched on to a group just starting to make its way through the rather grand entrance, flanked by four massive, carved stone elephants.

Inside, we found that although the brewery was beginning to fit the large stainless steel vats and pipe-work systems that are found in all modern breweries today, they still had a lot of the more traditional wooden equipment. As a result, we could still see some of the fermentation process taking place, which seemed to make the glasses of 'elephant' beer which we sampled at the end of the tour all the more satisfying. It was about the only thing that we did have time to sample as we continued our whistle-stop tour, but if we'd had a rough idea of what to expect when we visited Norway and Denmark, the same certainly couldn't be said about our last call on the trip.

We arrived in Helsinki three days later in bright sunshine. Finland was still feeling the effects of the 'Cold War' and at first our reception could have been described as much the same. Most Finns still had difficulty in making ends meet and there was still a lingering suspicion of anyone in uniform. The older generation was weary from years of disastrous war, followed by occupation and payment of reparations to the USSR. Even so, it was a source of pride that they had managed to pay it all off early. All this we had been told at the briefing we had received just before we arrived.

But it was in Helsinki that I met Paivi, and she wasn't like that at all.

The quayside where we docked ran alongside the edge of a square near the city centre. Soon after arriving, and when the ship had been spruced up a bit, we held an open day in a show of goodwill. We noticed straight away that though most of the older people stayed away, the younger ones, occasionally accompanied by their parents, descended on the ship in droves. It didn't take long to realise that they mostly just wanted to show off their smart and bright clothes. We were probably one of the first Western ships to visit the country for a long time and it was still something of a novelty.

Paivi came on board together with a couple of friends and I caught sight of her almost straight away. I was on one of the Bofors gun decks where I had been assigned to show visitors around. She was a bit shy and reserved in front of her friends, but I knew that as far as I was concerned she was going to be rather special. I had noticed that she wasn't at all Scandinavian-looking. Or so I thought at the time, but of course I learned later that Finns weren't all tall, blue-eyed, blonde Vikings and in fact they didn't think of themselves as Scandinavian at all.

She had long, auburn hair and was fairly tall, with large bones and a good figure. Her face was broad and open looking, and she had clear, well-separated, light green eyes and dark lashes. She was wearing a summery dress – nice but not really suitable for looking round ships. She was not much younger than I was – about eighteen or nineteen, I guessed. I didn't really notice her friends or what they looked like. I said hallo, and would she like to know all about the *Maidstone*. I said that it was about 500ft long and it displaced 9,000 tons. I wasn't sure if she would know how long a foot was, and I also doubted if they used tons in Finland, but I ploughed on.

I explained that it had a top speed of about 17 knots. I was pretty sure that she wouldn't know how fast that was but then I wasn't even really sure myself. I thought I might be on safer ground when I told her that it could supply and service a fleet of submarines when it was in combat, and that it originally had about sixteen anti-aircraft guns, similar to the one where we were.

All the while I had been trying to edge her away from the others, but to my disappointment, she wouldn't leave her friends. She seemed to be more interested in practicing her English than learning about guns or getting to know all about the navy, or even about me. But at least she seemed to be friendly. In the end, the best I could manage before they moved on to look at another part of the ship was a promise to meet me next day, to show me around Helsinki. We arranged to meet in the middle of the square nearby, which she told me was called something like Hietalahdenkatu. At the time I couldn't even pronounce it, let alone spell it.

I arrived early. At first I couldn't spot her and I began to think she wasn't coming. She probably just wanted to fob me off by promising to meet, I thought. Then, true to her word (and arriving alone I was glad to note) she appeared from across the square and walked towards me. She was dressed in a simple but attractive skirt and sweater. After having rather awkwardly greeted one another, we decided to make our way to one of the open-air cafés dotted around the edge of the square and when the waiter eventually wandered over to our table, she ordered two coffees. Then, while we waited for them to come, we 'broke the ice' with small talk.

I discovered that her name was Paivi and that she lived in an apartment no more than ten minutes walk away from where we were sitting. She was nearly nineteen years old and lived there with her sister and her mother who was the manageress of a clothes shop. Her father had seemingly been killed some years ago in the war, but I never discovered how and I thought it better not to ask.

Paivi would normally have been at the large department store a short tram ride away where she worked, but this week she was on holiday. That was how she had been able to come with her friends and see the ship. Her English was already pretty good and it got even better the more she spoke and the more she gained confidence. She had learned English in school she told me, but had also tried to learn from books and films. After a while, any signs of early embarrassment had disappeared and we settled into easy conversation. It wasn't until a second coffee had come and gone that the question of showing me around Helsinki came up again.

Like many teenagers in Finland, Paivi turned out to be not only extremely proud of Helsinki but a knowledgeable guide into the bargain. We caught a tram at the corner of the square and rattled our way to an area of the city about twenty minutes away, which I gathered was called Töölö. Then after a short walk, we approached the city's imposing Olympic stadium. Its slender tower at one end rose high above the giant white circular arena. Although built just before the war, it hadn't been properly utilised until the long-delayed summer games of 1952. Now it was used for concerts and major sporting events, Paivi told me. In fact, she had been to a concert there not long ago since, together with most of the other teenagers, Paivi preferred seeing the latest pop group rather than going to the concert hall with her mother and listening to Sibelius's music.

As there weren't any events taking place in the stadium at the time, we had to be content with admiring it from the outside. Afterwards, we boarded another tram back to the city centre, stopping off on the way to look at a couple of buildings by a Finnish architect called Alvar Aalto and to see the department store where Paivi worked. I had never heard of Alvar Aalto and didn't know much about architecture, but I could see from her enthusiasm that he was something of a hero in Finland. And I could at least appreciate that the buildings were modern, functional and simplistic, often with large flat or curved, unbroken lines.

On the other hand, the Stockmann department store where she worked was in a radically different style. Shopping wasn't really what I had in mind, but I had to admit that although the selection of goods on display wouldn't worry Bond Street, the building itself was built on a grand, traditional and impressive scale. It was much more decorative too – and more difficult to keep clean I thought, as I studied the outside.

Finally, we caught a ferry across to a popular restaurant on one of the several islands dotted around the harbour. I had discovered that although alcohol was strictly rationed and only available to locals at the Alko stores, being a visitor I was able to order a drink with our meal. I noticed that Paivi would only have a local version of soft drink and for this I was somewhat glad. Apart from anything else I remembered that I was a lowly paid national serviceman and that I was on a strict budget!

By the time we had finished our leisurely meal, trying all the while to ignore the curious glances from waiters and other diners, it was time to leave. We caught the ferry back to the mainland and by then we were holding hands. I walked her back to her apartment where she introduced me to her sister and mother. They seemed friendly enough, but a bit formal. Anxious for Paivi's welfare, I assumed. They didn't speak much English so conversation was a bit difficult and anyway, since I was due back on board ship, I didn't have much chance to stop and chat. There was just time for a brief farewell kiss with Paivi and another hurriedly arranged meeting in a couple of days' time.

I got back on board ship alright, but the next couple of days seemed to drag by. At last Thursday came and by twenty minutes past noon I had changed out of working clothes into my well-pressed No. 1 suit and had left the ship, forsaking any lunch. Paivi was waiting nearby and gave me a welcoming smile and a hug. Happily it seemed that she hadn't thought better of it in the intervening period. She slipped her arm through mine and soon we were back into our earlier intimacy and roles of tourist and guide. It was a fine, warm afternoon and when she suggested taking a ferry to one of the islands just off the coast outside Helsinki, I was happy to go along with her suggestion. At least, I thought, it might be a chance to be alone for a while, although I wasn't sure if that was what she had in mind.

It turned out that we were going to one of the favourite local tourist spots. The huge, ancient fortress at Suomenlinna was built on six interconnected islands and guarded the harbour entrance. It took about twenty minutes to get there; then for the next hour or so we wandered around the islands and the massive old fortress. The area was beginning to be used less as a munitions dump and defence fortification and more as a naval academy. There was also the beginnings of an artists' colony and it had become a highly sought after place to build a house. The fields surrounding the buildings were a popular place for picnics and we eventually tired of sightseeing and wandered away across the grassy slopes. We found a secluded spot in a warm, sunny hollow, lay on our backs in the warmth in contentment and lazily talked about our lives.

I realise now that I probably came on to her too quickly, but we would be leaving in a couple more days and I was in too much of a hurry. The first gentle kisses seemed to be welcomed and I should have been content with that – at least for a while. But I went too far, too quickly. The next thing I knew, she had struggled to her feet and said that we ought to get back to the ferry because the last one would be leaving soon. I didn't argue, but as I followed her, I was inwardly cursing. We stopped off for a meal, which was a little more subdued than usual and then I walked her home. This time I wasn't invited in, but we arranged to meet again for my last spot of leave before we had to depart in two days time. Things seemed to be alright again. We kissed before we said goodnight and I found my way through the tangle of streets and back to the ship.

Of course, she wasn't there as arranged. And I didn't go searching for her. Either it was because I was too proud, or maybe because I hadn't made a note of the address and thought I wouldn't be able to find her apartment again. We had been having a great time, and I felt let down. I wondered what had gone wrong. Maybe I had overstepped the mark. Maybe her mother had warned her about getting serious, or perhaps she already had a boyfriend and just didn't want it to go any further. I didn't know.

I wandered around for a while and then went back on board *Maidstone*. Helsinki didn't seem to hold any further interest for me. In time, of course, I realised that my romantic interlude in a foreign country was far from an unusual occurrence in the navy. That evening as I sat alone in the mess, I illogically still felt aggrieved.

But that wasn't quite the end of our visit. On the way home, we learned that there had been a reaction to our visit and our aim of spreading goodwill in Scandinavia had partly backfired. Accompanying us on the Helsinki part of the trip was an old aircraft carrier called HMS *Ocean* which, like us, was still just about seaworthy. As a fighting force, the two ships would have been hard-pressed to pose a threat to anyone, even if we had tried. So, we were more than a bit amused to learn on the way back home that the trip had caused something of a diplomatic stir. The Russians, who themselves had only recently pulled out of their last military base near Helsinki, had apparently complained that it had been an act of provocation on our part. We were pretty sure that the Finns, on the other hand, had breathed a sigh of relief when the occupying troops left, even though the Russians had claimed all along that they were only there for the Finns' own protection. At last, the people of Helsinki wouldn't have to lower the window blinds on trains any more as they went past the occupier's military base. At last they could call it their own country again.

For my part I didn't feel particularly provocative. I just felt disappointed and, perversely, probably a bit annoyed as well. I caught the train from Portland back to Pompey and made my way to HMS *Dolphin*. I had only been away for six or seven weeks so not much had changed. I was in a different mess this time but the regime was much the same. The usual round of cleaning out the mess, guard duty, lectures, cinema, kit inspections and trips into town on off-duty nights. The only things that seem to have changed were the personnel and by then it was something I had got used to. We were all resting after service on one boat or another and the old crews that I had known before had left once more. I did get a week's leave back home, but by now even that seemed to be part of the routine.

CHAPTER 12

FLEET EXERCISES

Spring was approaching and the Admiralty's thoughts naturally turned to a fleet 'exercise'. The Russians had been doing a bit of sabre rattling in the continuing Cold War exchanges and the military leaders thought it would be a good time for the fleet to flex its muscles in retaliation. The ice in the Barents Sea would soon be melting. It would release the Russian ships from their winter hibernation in northern ports and out into the slowly warming Arctic Ocean. A show of strength was obviously called for and a noticeable change came over the whole Home Fleet. Ships which had lain idle for several months in their home ports were given the navy's equivalent of a spring clean. Ships' tanks were filled with fuel and fresh water, stores were swung aboard by crane and anyone who was not involved in these tasks did their best to look busy anyway. That usually meant they went around with a paint brush or tin of polish in one hand.

Meanwhile I had been transferred again, this time to serve on my first submarine, HMS *Sturdy*. The contrast with what I had got used to on the *Maidstone* was little short of dramatic. At only 1,000 tons displacement it was one of the fleet's smaller S-class boats; only just over 70 yards in length and 7 yards wide. The crew consisted of less than fifty officers and men. It probably wasn't the smallest ship in the navy, but it didn't miss that distinction by much! By comparison to the *Sturdy*'s crew, a tin-full of Shipham sardines were probably quite comfortable!

Built in the early 1940s, the *Sturdy* had been launched too late to take part in any of the action in Europe during the Second World War. Instead, it had achieved a fairly distinguished record in the Far East, where it had been involved in the sinking of a large quantity of Japanese shipping. But by the time I went on board, the navy's ships were all beginning to show their age and in spite of a recent refit, the *Sturdy* was well past its sell-by-date. The top speed was little more than 15 knots on the surface and quite a bit less when it was submerged. It was one of five submarines (or 'boats' as the navy insisted on calling them), which would be accompanying the fleet to Gibraltar. We were all going to take part in a Mediterranean exercise which was scheduled to last for about six weeks.

Sturdy was equipped with two large diesel engines, known affectionately as 'grunt' and 'groan' by the stokers who had the pleasure of keeping them running, and it took most of the usual sea trials that followed a refit to finally get them running evenly – in addition, of course, to all the motors, pumps, compressors, refrigerators, generators and assorted machinery which were crammed into an operational submarine.

Before we left port, we manoeuvred a number of torpedoes down through the front hatch, putting four of them in the forward tubes, two in the aft, and the rest stowed away on their cradles in the torpedo space. This storage area, which was normally filled with two closely packed rows of occupied cradles, doubled up as a very uncomfortable mini-cinema for our occasional moments of relaxation. These usually occurred while we were in port or occasionally during long periods of travelling on the surface. Watching some Hollywood epic whilst sitting on or surrounded by a menacing array of torpedoes was something of an experience. This assumed, of course, that we had been able to get hold of some films in the first place, and that the projector was working!

After a few days spent clearing up all the loose equipment that had been left behind and abandoned during the refit, and having completed our sea trials, the captain announced to the rest of the fleet that we were ready to sail. Soon afterwards, the fleet admiral and most of his staff of captains and commanders appeared – seemingly from nowhere. Golf clubs were stowed away, gin bottles set aside and everyone dispersed to their various ships. For many, it was the first taste of the sea that they had had for some time and soon the fleet took on the atmosphere of a spring cruise. The ship's company (as the regular crews were called) soon appeared to be outnumbered by the visiting Admiralty staff!

Referring to all the gold braid on display, one of our electricians summed it up succinctly: 'There's more scrambled egg around here, boyo, than in a Forte's restaurant.' I wondered vaguely where they all managed to sleep. It was my first proper large-scale exercise, since previously I had only been on short trips where we had taken the part of an enemy ship for the RAF to use us as simulated targets.

But before we finally left home waters and the exercise could begin, there was one more treat in store for us. We set off from the quayside and soon afterwards the recently commissioned Royal Yacht *Britannia* hove into sight ahead. On board was the newly appointed Admiral of the Fleet, Prince Philip, together with the Queen. While the ship stayed firmly at anchor (the Queen was rumoured to be a reluctant sailor, even in calm seas) they stood together with the captain and other important guests on a large wooden platform rigged up beneath a canvas canopy on the foredeck. The plan was that our submarine, soon to be followed by the motley of assembled ships, would sail past one at a time and pay their respects. Like many other royal occasions, it had been carefully rehearsed in their absence during the previous few days.

As we approached *Britannia*, the *Sturdy's* entire crew (except for anyone actually involved in controlling the boat) stood to attention in a row along the upper casing. All of us were dressed in our best No. 1 going ashore suits. Then, on getting closer – close enough to see the Duke and officials all saluting and the Queen mustering up a dignified pose – our 'Jimmy' called out over the tannoy: 'Three cheers for Her Majesty the Queen. Hip, hip –' We dutifully followed his bidding with a loud cry of 'hooray', which rang out across the intervening waters, at the same time removing our caps between the thumb and forefinger of the right hand and waving them in the air in a clockwise direction. All-in-all, it was a great show of well-rehearsed spontaneity!

Travelling on the surface we would have reached Gibraltar in about six days. But on the morning of the third day, we brought the engines to slow and went up on deck while waiting for the rest of the fleet to catch up. The exercise involved us creeping up on a large, unsuspecting ship following on somewhere behind. The ship would be protected by several shadowing destroyers but we had been instructed to attempt a simulated attack. It turned out to be the same HMS *Maidstone* that I had been serving on just a few weeks before.

Following nearly two hours of aimlessly searching the ocean, the lookout on the bridge at last spotted a small cloud of smoke on the horizon. The skipper decided that this was what we had been waiting for and, at his command, we all made a hasty dash for the conning tower hatch. Then, having first checked that everyone else had gone below, he slammed shut the hatch cover and secured the retaining clips holding it fast. It was rumoured that on a previous occasion he had called for the engines to be stopped and the boat had even started to dive before he learned that there were still two sailors left on deck.

Happily, this time we all managed to get below safely before the klaxon sounded for all hands to take up their action stations. In my case, that meant a small, noisy and cramped space between decks, where I operated the pumps controlling the buoyancy of the submarine once it was below the surface. Another scream of the klaxon sounded through the confined space of the engine room, above the deafening noise of the machinery, and before it had died away a wild, cursing melee of bodies erupted through-out the length and breadth of the boat. Some of the half-dressed crew members had been off-duty, resting or asleep and they hastily pulled on the remainder of their clothing and hurried to their allotted action station. The chief petty officer and his leading stoker rushed over to close the fuel shut-off valves in the engine room. This cut off the fuel and oil supplies to 'grunt' and 'groan' and the engines came to a halt immediately.

More stokers arrived from the mess room and helped to close down the group exhaust valves and shut off the muffler valves, quickly followed by the engine compression cocks. We could now disconnect the engine clutches and the propellers would be connected through the shaft to the electric motor turning gear located in the motor room. Meanwhile electricians were pulling out switches and pushing in circuit breakers to stop charging the batteries and switch the power to run the electric motors instead.

In the control room there was the same scene of hectic activity. The control panel operators pulled the dive handles to open the main vents. Almost immediately the ballast tanks along the sides of the submarine started filling up and in less than a minute from the first blast of the klaxon, we had sunk beneath the waves. Fans were switched off, as were most of the lights. All noise and use of electricity was cut to the absolute minimum. In the fore ends last-minute adjustments were made to the torpedoes. The long weeks of practice drill seemed to have paid off.

In the control room, the hydroplane operators held the boat on an even keel and kept the needle of the large, semi-circular depth gauge at 45ft. The attack team were all at their stations throughout the boat and everyone was keyed up for the coming engagement. The skipper clasped the handles of the raised periscope as he peered into its eyepieces and did a complete 360-

degree scan of the sea above. A small circle of blue light reflected in his eyes as he concentrated on what was happening above. The only other light in the control room was from the dim red glow of a naked bulb overhead.

Finally the skipper seemed satisfied with what he had seen. He knocked up the steadying handles and stepped back. Immediately an operator who was seated nearby pulled a lever at the side of the control panel and the periscope sank silently downwards into its tube in the floor. 'One hundred feet,' the skipper called, and the hydroplane operator swung the handlebar-like levers in response.

When the gauge needle was showing the correct depth, I got a quiet command over the loudspeaker in my cramped attack position to operate the ballast tank pumps and bring the boat level again. Another quiet call of 'close up for going deep' passed along the boat. Meanwhile, the compensating gauges and all the water inlet valves were closed off. The only lines left open were those that helped to cool the electric motors. That was in case we needed them in a hurry in order to dive deeper.

The only sounds inside the boat were the clicks of the hydrofoil gear as it followed the operator's movements, together with the soft whine of the motors and the ASDIC operator's voice as he softly called out the bearings of the approaching ships above. The loudest sound throughout the submarine was the swish of the propellers outside the hull as they churned through the seas.

The thought crossed my mind that if I could hear the noise of the propellers clearly, then perhaps others could as well. My fears were soon answered and it became apparent that they could! There were three loud thumps, as the frigate overhead dropped grenades in the water to let us know that we had been detected. It also meant that they could claim a 'kill'.

The grenades landed around the top of the outer casing of the boat and as they exploded, the shock waves made the submarine shudder from end to end.

HMS *Sturdy* was an old boat and even after her refit was not in the best of condition. The first grenade managed to stop the refrigerator; the second cracked a joint in the cooling water inlet pipe, spraying liquid all over the engines. The third somehow blew small holes in various parts of the fresh water supply line, causing little cascades of water to suddenly appear all over the boat. Crockery slid off the mess table and smashed on the deck. Bodies thrashed about cursing in pain as they fell against hard machinery and steelwork in the semi-darkness. 'It's a bloody good thing they were using grenades and not depth charges,' muttered 'Candles' Malone, when he had stopped swearing.

'Candles' had acquired his nickname whilst serving on a previous boat. Having fired a smoke candle from underwater to let a ship above know that they had been detected and 'sunk', he had opened up the breach to find that the candle was stuck inside. It was also still alight, having been ignited by the seawater when the outside watertight door had been opened. He then famously carried it, still smoking fiercely, to the captain and asked innocently, 'What shall I do with this sir, I think it's still burning?' By that time, the boat was engulfed in smoke and everyone was in a state of panic, not knowing what had happened. Half of the crew had gone to the front of the boat and had started to don escape suits.

The captain, who was not a man to normally lose his temper, exploded: 'Get rid of the bloody candle, you maniac.' Moving quickly to the control panel, he started to operate several valve handles, blowing air into all the ballast tanks and getting the boat immediately to the surface. The candle was finally extinguished in the bilges and the nickname 'Candles' stuck for evermore! Needless to say, he wasn't allowed to operate the underwater gun again.

Our exercise and simulated attack lasted another three hours. We fired off a couple of torpedoes fitted with dummy warheads and set at sufficient depth to pass well below their targets and hopefully not hit them. Then while the rest of the fleet went off to search for the now floating, reusable main bodies of the torpedoes, we surfaced and headed for Gibraltar. The word was passed through the boat to 'stand down'.

Relaxing later in what passed for our mess, with a well-earned tot of rum, I had just finished my drink when Sid Evans, who was part of the attack team, returned from the control room. 'Let's have mine, quick mun,' he pleaded. 'I see you've all managed to finish before I got back. Well, don't expect any of mine. While you lot have all been sitting around drinking, some of us have been working you know,' he added.

There were cries of dismay. 'Oh, we've forgotten about Sid. We thought you weren't coming, Sid, so we drunk yours.'

'The lot of you had better just watch out for yourselves, if you have. Now give it here, before I clear the lot of you.'

Since Sid was well over 6ft tall and weighed about 14 or 15 stone, his drink was quickly found and put into his hand. We waited until he had lowered the level in the glass to about half full with the first swallow before someone asked Sid how the attack had gone, not having seen any of the action himself from his position down aft.

'No fear of hitting anything, I suppose?' the questioner enquired, 'I heard that the skipper couldn't hit the *Queen Mary* from the inside. He must be cross-eyed or something.'

'More likely he was drunk,' someone else remarked.

'You won't believe this,' said Sid slowly, 'but we actually hit something this time.'

He waited for his incredible news to sink in and the cries of incredulity to die down.

'I'm telling you, he did,' he said. 'He hit the *Albion*.'

'Mind you,' he continued, starting to grin. 'The thing is mun, we were aiming at the *Maidstone* and the *Albion* was a good half a mile away.'

The navy tradition of issuing a daily ration of 'pussers tot' to its serving crews dated back more than 300 years. Senior ratings were allowed to drink their tot neat, but as junior ratings we were supposed to dilute it with two parts of water to one of rum. As it quickly went off, this was supposed to prevent it being stored and drunk with other hoarded supplies on another day.

Although it was generally known as 'Jamaican' rum, the liquor was in fact a mixture from two Caribbean sources as well as from Trinidad. At the time, we each had a tot card; it was almost as valuable as our passbook. The two were generally kept together in a navy-issue plastic wallet, and entitled us to our daily ration. The ceremony of ladling out the total quantity for each mess into its own rum bucket, before serving it to each individual rating, was taken very seriously. Tradition dictated that the person whose turn it was to ladle out the rations should in return be proffered 'wets' or 'sippers' from everyone's drink. It was completely against naval rules, of course, and anybody who was foolish enough to accept the twenty or thirty proffered 'wets' regretted it afterwards.

Naval rum didn't really taste the same as the commercial variety, it was something of an acquired taste, but naturally I had managed to acquire it before the completion of my service. Strangely, after I left the service, I never drank it again and in any case I wasn't really surprised when, to some people's dismay, the practice was brought to an end in 1970. The rum was over 50 per cent proof and with everyone getting an eighth of a pint before water was added, it had certainly helped to keep the lower ranks happy. On the other hand, I doubt if it had improved their sobriety or efficiency. The old sea shanty 'What shall we do with the drunken sailor?' could strike a chord with many a serviceman even then, though to be strictly correct we were probably seamen and not 'sailors'. When you considered the hardships that most sailors went through in times gone by, it was pretty understandable, but the tradition didn't seem to have any place in the modern, efficient navy.

Back on the *Sturdy*, we finished our break and went back on duty. Leaving the other ships behind, we broke off from the exercise and made our way on the surface to Gibraltar, reaching it a couple of days later. Eventually the skipper found a place to tie up in the crowded dockyard and we lost no time in checking over the boat to see what damage had resulted from our encounter with the grenade-dropping frigate. Luckily, it turned out to be fairly minor and only took a day or so to carry out the necessary repairs. The small leaks from joints, valve connections and gauges were much less serious than we had at first thought and the refrigerator was also soon working again.

Once all the work had been finished, we had time to relax and look around. Unfortunately, it didn't take long to discover that there wasn't much to do in Gibraltar and what there was didn't take very long to do. 'The Rock', as most people called it, was only about three miles long and less than a mile wide, so it didn't take very long to walk round it either. It was rather like a rocky gruyere cheese; a large lump of limestone sticking out into the sea and overlooking the entrance to the Mediterranean. The surface was riddled with caves and tunnels that now served as stores, gun emplacements, petrol and ammunition dumps. Together with a large dockyard, most of the land belonged to the military, and as such it was mostly off-limits to all but a few permanently based staff.

We soon found that once you had walked the length of the high street, fed the gangs of marauding and smelly Barbary apes, admired the rain collection system and gazed across the causeway and border to the town of Algeciras in Spain (also off-limits), we had exhausted most of the options. The Spanish didn't want us because we wouldn't give up Gibraltar to them and the Barbary apes, who seemed to be everywhere, didn't really approve of us either. We soon discovered that if you didn't have any peanuts to give them, they spitefully tried to bite you instead – which could not only be pretty painful, but was dangerous to your health as well!

What little nightlife there was to be had was already bagged by the thousand or so British and American matelots who had arrived before us and unless you wanted to get into a fight or play football at the barracks, there weren't many other distractions. In the end, the rest of our stay in Gibraltar passed without incident – unless, of course, you count the trouble over the moose's head, and that was only partly our fault.

The skipper had triumphantly appeared one day at the gangplank bearing a giant, stuffed moose's head. He had apparently discovered it in among a pile of discarded items at the back of the officers' mess. We looked on in disbelief as he bore the huge, dusty, moth-eaten prize aboard, although we had to admit that from a distance it looked quite impressive with its magnificent set of antlers.

Carrying it on board was one thing, but getting it down below deck proved to be quite another. Eventually the problem was solved by sawing off the antlers and fitting a set of steel locating pins into their base. This would allow the antlers to be removed separately for carrying aboard. A team of sailors was then detailed with a vacuum cleaner to smarten the trophy up, only to find to their horror that the animal's fur was being removed by the machine and it was rapidly becoming bald. Some quick thinking and the judicious use of glue and shoe polish eventually made it look smart enough to pass a casual glance. Finally we erected a frame in the conning tower on which to mount it.

Once floodlighting had been added, the captain could proudly show it off at night time in all its glory. His idea was that it would become the boat's mascot and while we were at sea it would reside down in the officers' wardroom. Only when we were in port would it be mounted up on the bridge on its frame where all could see. It could become a key talking point during visitors' days, for instance, and was certainly a feather in the skipper's cap.

And there the whole thing would probably have ended if someone hadn't gone and mentioned it to the local newspaper. The first we knew about it was when a photographer and reporter turned up at the quayside one morning and started taking pictures of the boat with the moose's head showing in the foreground. Then the reporter made his way on board and asked to speak with the captain. He was shown the way down to the Jimmy's quarters and didn't re-emerge for some time, eventually making his way back on deck accompanied by the skipper himself. A little later we discovered what had passed between them.

We were off duty, sitting and chatting in the mess, when we heard the warning, 'Look out, the Jimmy's coming'. A moment later he appeared in the hatchway entrance.

'Macdonald,' he said to Steve, 'we want you to help us out.' The emphasis on 'we' didn't escape us.

'Now look, no arguments! That is, if you don't want to be put on a charge,' he added, half jokingly. 'The thing is, I couldn't very well tell that reporter chappie exactly where we got the moose from or that I found it on a rubbish dump, could I?' he went on. 'So I told him that you nabbed it when you were on leave out hunting in Canada. I want you to think up a good story about catching it. It'll be good for the boat,' he ended lamely.

Steve Macdonald may have had a North American accent but to think that he was some sort of Canadian Davy Crockett was, to say the least, something of an exaggeration. He had spent his early years in Toronto, but later his family had moved back to Manchester and it was from there that he eventually signed up for the navy.

We all thought that it might be wiser to go along with the captain's wishes, so in the end Steve did think up a good story – or rather we all clubbed together and thought one up for him. It was a beauty if I do say it myself. It seemed to grow and grow until we had to cut it down a bit, as everyone thought up a new twist to the tale. It was more James Bond than Davy Crockett by the time we had finished! The dangers that Steve faced in order to get a mascot for his mates would have daunted most men. Steve eventually told the finished tale to the reporter, who went off a happy man, only to reappear later that day with his editor and the mayor. In fact, half the town bigwigs seemed to have turned up to see the celebrity.

Unfortunately, the first person they met at the quayside and making his way back on board was an ordinary stoker, who had been ashore all day and knew nothing of Steve's amazing bravery in tracking down and overpowering the moose. To make things worse, the stoker had been drinking rather a lot as well.

'Wha', tha' ole thing?' he managed to reply to their questions. 'Ooh, the Jimmy foun' it on a rubbis' dump.'

Luckily, the story hadn't yet got on to the presses, so it never actually got into print. On the other hand, the captain wasn't amused. He didn't seem to share everyone else's view of the incident. The moose's head mysteriously disappeared from its mounting frame that night and it wasn't mentioned again. There wasn't much mystery about Steve's stoppage of shore leave for a week, or that of the innocent stoker.

CHAPTER 13

PARTY TIME IN TANGIER

It may have been just a lucky coincidence but before the week was up we had an excuse to leave Gibraltar and set sail once more. Either it was to cut down on the number of fights taking place in the town or perhaps it was just in an unexpected act of generosity, but the Admiralty had decided to send us off on a goodwill visit across the straits to Tangier Some of the more cynical of the crew reckoned it was more likely to have been a tactical withdrawal to save face! But, for whatever reasons, we quickly decided that, compared to our last port of call, the temptations to be found in that particular part of the North African coast would be much more inviting. We felt that there were bound to be far more opportunities to get into some serious trouble!

I had realised by now that my knowledge of the world outside was fairly rudimentary and it certainly didn't include Tangier. My expertise extended to a vague feeling that tangerines may have come from there, but I wasn't even sure about that. By the time we left Tangier a couple of days later, I was still none the wiser about the origin of tangerines. On the other hand my education had been enhanced in other directions.

It was the late 1950s and Tangier was still classed as an 'International Zone'. In effect, that meant that it was a free port, with a pretty loose arrangement of taxation and 'sympathetic' financial and legal structures. The untidy town wouldn't get its independence for another couple of years. Until then, it still managed to be a playground for the Western world's dropouts. It made for a colourful mixture of eccentric millionaires and what were known in the navy as 'bum-boys'.

The town cafés, we were told, were known as the world's meeting-house for international spies. They were a Mecca for speculators and gamblers alike. At the time, the seedy (some said exotic) streets were a haven for writers and artists seeking a whiff of inspiration. Since it was the sort of place where everything was available if you had the money, and often when you didn't, it was more likely that they were just there for relaxation.

Our boat came slowly into the harbour and eventually drew up alongside two other submarines that were already tied up against the sea wall. It seemed that we were not going to be the only ones on this particular outing, but if anyone on board had thought that our visit was going to be some sort of holiday, we were soon to discover otherwise. The gang planks had hardly been laid across to the other boats, than the job of spring-cleaning began.

The next couple of days were spent sprucing up the boat ready to receive the various dignitaries who had been invited to pay a visit. The machinery was wiped down, the brass work was polished, buckets of sea water were sloshed over the decks and everything was swept down or tided up. I was beginning to think that if it was true that an army marched on its stomach, then the navy must sail with a tin of Brasso.

The following Sunday morning, we had dressed in our best uniforms as assorted local consulate staff, diplomatic corps and wives clambered across the gangplanks and disappeared down below. All morning the three submarines were a hive of activity and, as instructed, we had remained on our best behaviour. Finally, just before lunchtime, everyone was able to breathe a sigh of relief as the last visitor left. There was an even greater feeling of elation when, soon afterwards, we heard that the officers would be attending a party ashore that evening at the Governor's house and we could have the rest of the day off to relax. Over lunch, while everyone else thought about how they could spend their unex-pected break ashore, some members of the crew were making plans to hold their own impromptu party on board.

Steve and I had ambled off into town to explore. We knew noth-ing of the alternative arrangements being made back on the boat. We finally weakened before the barrage of guides who wanted to show us the sights of Tangiers and we picked out a student who spoke a little English and said he could show us around for the rest of the afternoon. Once selected, he immediately shouted in Arabic to the noisy crowd of following children, pimps and hangers-on and sent them on their way.

Guided by Ali (or so it turned out was his name), we slowly wound our way through crowded streets, past some of the shops and into the old square at Grand Socco. Having persuaded him that we didn't want to see where 'Tennis He (sic) Williams had lived', we told him instead that we wanted to go somewhere different, and not where he always took tourists.

We spent the next half an hour listening in fascination to Ali bargain with the local taxi drivers for their best fares. Finally, he seemed satisfied with the price that one of them quoted and we bumped along the roads in an ancient taxi for a while, until we reached the Caves of Hercules. We had gathered from various sources that these ancient caverns cut into cliff-sides overlooking the Atlantic coast, although not having now been occupied for centuries, were still well worth a visit. Ali had assured us that they were only a short drive outside the town.

Unfortunately, of course, we had forgotten to check the times of the tides. By the time we arrived, it turned out to be nearly high tide and by that time the entrance was nearly covered by the sea. Unable to get inside, we had to be satisfied with viewing from afar instead. Having purchased the mandatory postcards from a nearby stall, we climbed into the ancient taxi and trundled back along the track into town. We paid off our guide, bid him goodbye and found somewhere to have a meal and a couple of drinks instead.

It was approaching ten o'clock and had been dark for some time when we made our way back to the boat. The officers' party had already ended and some of those on early shift had returned to the boat. I noticed that we were now tied up to the sea wall, since the other two submarines must have left during the afternoon. I also noticed that someone was waiting for us to come on board. We met Joe at the after hatch. He seemed a bit agitated.

'Here,' he whispered urgently. 'You gotta give us a hand.' That made us suspicious straight away.

'We have to get a couple of skirts ashore without them being seen. We had a bit of a party this afternoon like, and they were hanging around on the quayside so we invited them to come and join us. I think the Jimmy is a bit suspicious. He's up on the bridge and the quartermaster's snooping around the deck as well. He's been round twice already.'

The captain of a ship was often confusingly called a 'Jimmy'. But it was even more confusing in our case since, as the senior officer-in-charge of a submarine like ours rarely held the rank of a full-blown captain, the 'captain' on the *Sturdy* actually had the rank of a lieutenant commander.

'What!' exclaimed Steve, 'How the hell did you get women on board the boat?'

'Well,' Joe grinned, innocently. 'You know how it is. It was easy with all them visitors wandering around, and a few of the women seemed to want to stay. Cor, it's like a brothel down there!'

I got the distinct impression that he thought it was a bit of a laugh, and didn't quite appreciate the trouble we would all be in if they were caught.

'You'd better get them off somehow,' we told him firmly. 'And quickly too, or we're in real trouble.'

'We've been trying to,' he assured us. 'But the Jimmy will see them if we take them off by the for'ard gangway and the aft gangway has been taken away. I reckon he's suspicious and he's keeping an eye on what's going on. Got any ideas?' he asked hopefully.

We kept in the shadows whilst considering the problem, trying not to attract attention. It was Steve who finally came up with the idea.

'We need to create a diversion,' he said. 'It's got to be down at the front of the boat so you can smuggle the girls off by the gangway while everyone's attention is somewhere else. Joe, you'll just have to fall overboard. But don't forget, it's got to be right at the front end and on the seaward side.'

Joe didn't think much of the idea at first, but he couldn't come up with any alternative, so in the end he relented and that was what we did. I doubt that he would have agreed at all if he wasn't half-cut and if I hadn't happily assured him that it was the only way of helping him out of trouble. He looked down at the dark waters of the harbour below, and hastily moved back from the edge. It was only after Steve had once again assured him that we would help get the women off while he was making his brave sacrifice that he doubtfully made his way forward, all the time keeping out of sight of the bridge. 'I hope the lads realise what I am doing for them,' was his parting shot.

We waited expectantly. For a few more minutes nothing happened. Then there was a cry, followed quickly by a splash and the sound of someone thrashing around in the water. To the accompaniment of loud cries for help, Joe gave his impressive imitation of a drowning man and for the next five minutes there was chaos on board. Everyone, including the captain I was pleased to note, rushed forward to help. That was our cue to help the partially clad ladies up the after hatch and across the now unattended gangway. Soon they had disappeared into the night, clutching their earnings and their belongings.

While we congratulated ourselves on the success of our subterfuge, they fished Joe out of the sea. The next day he had a temperature of 106 and, to make things worse, he discovered later that he had caught a dose as well.

'And I thought she was decent too,' he said disgustedly. 'It just goes to show you can't trust anyone!'

★★★

Our visit to Tangier was scheduled to be only for a few days. Just before we were due to leave, the daily orders indicated that there would be a reception on board the submarine in honour of the local consulate staff. It was by way of returning their hospitality and would round off our visit nicely. Those of us who weren't on duty that afternoon and were lucky enough not to have been volunteered for the job of waiters or general helpers, were expected to be well out of the way. Instead we were given five hours of leave ashore, together with strict instructions to be back before midnight.

With the captain's advice to keep out of trouble, keep together in groups and to seek the services of a reliable guide, studiously ignored, we set off in the growing darkness towards the nearby town. Apart from the Grand Socco, where we'd been before, there didn't seem to be a centre to the town and we found ourselves entering a maze of narrow side streets instead. We had no idea of where we were going, but we were determined to find our own way to wherever it was.

In retrospect it may have been a mistake to join up with Steve and Ronnie and head for what we thought was the old part of the town. Ronnie had assured us that he knew the way to the Casbah square and the old Sultan's Palace. Then Steve said we were wasting valuable drinking time while we strolled around the main shopping areas.

Instead, we struck off into a maze of narrow, ill-lit alleyways and headed towards what seemed to be the Arab quarter. After a while, we realised that we had no idea where we were, but at least it had thrown off most of the potential guides who had been pestering us with their offers to show us a 'good time'. We appeared to have ended up in some sort of souk or bazaar, with cafés, small market stalls and hole-in-the-wall shops that displayed a bewildering array of carpets, leather goods, pots and pans, wood carvings and bags of spices.

The next hour or so was spent haggling prices for small silver and leather presents to take home. This involved a lot of hand signals and gesticulating, since nobody knew a word of the other's language. In the end, pure commercial acumen seemed to decide the end result and although we were certain that our skill and determination had won the day, in fact we probably could have got everything a lot cheaper if we had been more experienced at haggling. Clutching our 'bargains' we wandered on, looking for anywhere that seemed to offer the promise of lively action.

We wandered on, getting further and further from the relative bustle of the souks and beginning to feel a bit conspicuous. We tried to keep in the middle of the narrow streets, avoiding any deep shadows and wondering what form any trouble would take. A sudden rattle behind us, as the metal shutters of a café were noisily closed for the night, nearly made us jump out of our skin.

Eventually, we headed thankfully for a bar that we spied up ahead and found an empty table in a dingy, sweet smelling, smoke-laden area just off the main alleyway. Then, trying to ignore the inquisitive stares from all around and, with a mixture of sign language and a few badly pronounced Arabic drinking terms that Ronnie had somehow picked up over the years, we ordered some local beers.

Several beers later, the atmosphere around us appeared to have become a bit more relaxed. The locals had accepted our presence and the barman who had been serving us came over to our table. By now we realised he knew some English and so we weren't too surprised when after a few pleasantries, he eventually got round to asking us if we wanted a bit more fun. Not knowing quite what to expect, we cautiously said that we might. Bidding us to follow him, he led us over to where we had noticed people appearing from and disappearing periodically behind a curtain.

Narrow, winding stairs led downwards and we could hear the sound of music coming from somewhere below. We followed him through another curtain-covered doorway and, as he opened the door behind, the loud whining sound of an Arab group of musicians burst upon us. We entered a fairly large, cellar-like room, much like the one we had left, but noisier, smokier and with a lot of scantily dressed women standing around. Three of them immediately detached themselves from the bar as we were shown to a table at the side of the musicians. In front was a small, cleared area where a belly dancer slowly gyrated. The three girls came over and, possibly because of a shortage of chairs, promptly sat on our laps. We noticed that while our attention was being distracted by their effusive greetings, a couple of bottles of cheap-looking champagne and a number of glasses had mysteriously appeared on our table.

In spite of the language barrier, we rapidly made friends with everyone, especially the girls. Soon the tempo of the music increased, together with its volume and the musicians went into what turned out to be the final climax, beating out an almost hypnotic rhythm that was soon accompanied by the frenzied encouragement of the audience. Sweat was breaking out on the dancer's face; her eyes rolling in unison with her exertions. Gasping now for breath, the belly dancer abandoned herself to the music, her legs thrust open wide, everything gyrating and shaking, arms coiling and waving wildly, her body going rubbery as it bent double and swayed. She continued to shake even as her ample bosom broke loose from its restraints. With stomach and bottom gyrating madly, and with the drums beginning to roll, the buttons holding a scanty skirt around her hips suddenly burst open under the strain and everything fell to the floor. I wondered if this was all part of the act, but in any case it brought the show to a spectacular end. The music stopped and, gathering up her few clothes from the floor, the dancer made a half-hearted attempt to cover herself up.

The buxom dancer sauntered around the tables, accepting money and friendly smacks on her well-upholstered bottom with equal enjoyment from the wildly cheering crowd. She held one hand across her chest while the other was carrying her clothes and I soon realised it was not from any sense of modesty, but more to create a deep cleavage into which the spectators could thrust folded money.

Steve invited her over to our table and more bottles of champagne appeared. It was at about this time that we began to notice three things; the first of which was that it was already well past midnight. Next, we began to realise that several empty champagne bottles had materialised on the table without either having been ordered or the contents drunk. And then the most worrying thing we noticed was that some of the women weren't women at all.

We decided it was time to leave, but understandably there was then a disagreement over who had ordered all the champagne and who should pay for it. Later, I became a bit confused over what followed, but there was definitely a lot of shouting, tables were overturned and glasses smashed. Several people, including ourselves it must be said, started fighting and some of the women (I assumed afterwards that it was the genuine women, but I can't be sure) were screaming.

I heard Ronnie shout 'Let's get out of here' and we all dashed for the stairs and the street outside. How we found our way back to the boats is still something of a mystery, but I gathered later that as we were being chased down an alleyway, we were extremely fortunate to run into a group of ex-pats who had been out celebrating at a nearby club. On seeing that they were outnumbered, the pursuers seemed to mysteriously disappear. Luckily, once we had explained our predicament, the group of newly found friends insisted on showing us the way back to the boat. It was then that we realised just how far we had wandered off the main streets, but eventually we began to recognise some of the streets and soon the welcome sight of the *Sturdy* lay ahead. It was well past midnight. We gratefully thanked our ex-pat saviours, filed sheepishly back on board under the watchful eye of the quartermaster and went below to the mess as quietly as possible.

Next morning, we found ourselves on 'defaulters' and ended up in front of the captain for being late off leave. There didn't seem much point in brazening it out, and we thought openness would be the best policy. We all admitted that we had no excuse, but to our surprise the Jimmy almost immediately told us to go away and come back when we could provide a good reason for our tardiness. Ten minutes later we returned to his cabin and stood in line at attention as best we could in the cramped space.

'Well?' he barked out, 'What have you got to say for yourselves. It would have served you right if we had sailed without you.'

'Sir, the reason we were late,' said Steve, whom we had appointed as spokesman, 'was that the taxi that we had caught in plenty of time had a crash, and after we had waited to give statements to the police about the accident, we had to walk back the rest of the way and we ended up late.'

We felt sure that the story contained just the right amount of civic duty and ring of truth about it. But the captain had other ideas. He was an old hand and had heard all the excuses from errant sailors before. He remained silent for a moment, apparently thinking it over, while we waited expectantly.

'You're a bunch of bloody liars,' he snapped out at last. 'Three days stoppage of leave and pay. Dismissed.'

Chapter 14

Maltese Cross

We cast off from Tangier and proceeded on the surface into the heart of the Mediterranean proper. Once we were well away from any land we dived to about 50ft below the waves and spent the next two or three days playing cat and mouse with the rest of the NATO fleet. The skipper loosed off a few more torpedoes and though he was a little more successful than before, our score of 'hits' remained impressively low.

One consolation was that although our hit rate wouldn't impress anyone, we didn't have to put up with any more grenades being dropped on us. I'm not sure whether it was because no one could find us or whether they were afraid that we might sink. During our short stay in Tangier we had done some more hasty repairs to all of the leaking joints we could find, but we didn't have time to test them. Happily, the remainder of the practice passed off without event and at the end of the exercise we headed for Malta, glad to be travelling on the surface for a change and with the main hatches open.

A spell of travelling on the surface was always a welcome break for us, particularly if the sea was flat and calm. Apart from the chance to move around a bit, you also noticed that if we had been snorkelling just below the surface for some time – or even if we had been running deep for a while on the electric motors – it got pretty stuffy down below. Against this, you had to balance the fact that it was usually a lot calmer below the surface, particularly if the seas above were choppy. Most of the time it was a bit like travelling in a narrow metal tube, where you could nearly touch the sides of the mess by merely stretching out your arms and you knew that the sea was all around you and only a few feet away.

With the lack of space and the shortage of bunks in the cramped quarters, we had to use a system of 'hot bunking'. It meant that we had to share beds alternatively with the rest of the crew in a four hours on-four hours off rota. Not only were we in the same clothes most of the time, but even catching up on some sleep or eating food had to be done during the four hours that we were off watch. To put it politely, after a fortnight at sea even your best friends began to niff.

As a part of the refit back in Pompey the 'dockies', as they were disparagingly known in the navy, had thoughtfully fitted the *Sturdy* with a fresh water shower. They weren't to know that fresh water was a far too precious commodity on a submarine to waste it having a bath or a shower. As a result, the object of all their labours just stood there unused. There was an alternative seawater shower on board, but its use wasn't all that popular. There was little in the way of personal privacy on board a submarine and in spite of the shower having a sort of half curtain, you would have to wash right in the middle of a bunch of working sailors. In any case, seawater was pretty hopeless for washing in and added to that there always seemed to be lots of potentially painful, sharp-edged machines nearby to contend with!

I soon found that trying to maintain any sort of long-term bodily hygiene could be both an irksome and an uncomfortable task. There weren't any proper facilities for washing or drying clothes either and since there was hardly any locker space to store things, most people only brought one change of clothes with them. So, despite having some oxygen replenishment equipment which we could use during prolonged dives, and though it was often quieter and calmer below the surface, we all looked forward to breathing fresh air again. It was then that you realised how stale the air inside the boat had become – and also who your real friends were!

We stopped for a while in the empty sea, with the strong Mediterranean sun blazing down from a clear sky and a loud cheer went up when the skipper announced over the tannoy that we could all take a bathing break. Dignity and rank were ignored as everyone began stripping off clothes that they had probably been wearing for the last couple of weeks. The air was filled with whoops of pleasure as everyone in the boat began jumping and diving from the casing down into the turquoise waters. We soon found out that it wasn't quite as warm as we had imagined, but after several days at sea it was still something of a luxury and we quickly got used to the temperature. An hour later, we started up the engines again and set course for Malta.

Running at a steady 10 knots, we reached our destination by the next day. I happened to be off watch and relaxing on deck as we approached the entrance to the Grand Harbour at Valletta. At first sight, the seemingly barren island was something of a disappointment. The town of Valletta stood on top of a steep, rocky entrance and was surrounded by a sprawl of rather sad-looking houses and buildings. Grand Harbour on the other hand, proved to be a far more impressive sight. A deep-water entrance and high, rocky tributaries seemed to be cut into the very city itself.

Guarding the left-hand side of the harbour mouth was the rather imposing-looking building of Fort Saint Angelo. Away in the distance we could make out what was left of the original, now bombed-out entrance to the town. It was almost as if it had been left as a stark reminder of what the islanders had endured during the Second World War, less than fifteen years earlier.

Manoeuvring a ship or boat into a busy harbour for the first time was always a challenge. I wasn't sure whether our skipper had been there before, but I did know that it was always a difficult time for anyone unlucky enough to be on duty on the bridge at the same time. The skipper considered the bridge to be his own exclusive territory and he guarded over it jealously. Anyone who was foolish enough to question any decision of his or to get in his way or cross his path was unceremoniously ordered off the bridge.

That morning as usual, he was dashing from one side of the bridge to the other, cursing and waving his fists at any small boat or yacht which came within a hundred yards of us. He dared them at their peril to get in our way. The skipper ignored the fact that, as a comparatively small craft fitted with twin engines, we were in fact reasonably manoeuvrable inside the harbour and should, in fact, give way to anything less manoeuvrable. He always maintained that if he merely set a course straight for where he wanted to go, everyone else should automatically get out of his way. If for any reason they didn't, then he would just stand and bellow at them until they did.

Very occasionally he would succumb to using the code of the sea and actually signalled his intentions to any other ships nearby, using the required number of blasts on the ship's siren. Unfortunately, it was almost certain that whoever received the order from him would probably be too nervous to carry it out correctly. It happened again on this occasion.

'Who the hell does that tanker think he is?' shouted out the skipper. 'He could see I was going that way and he still carried on. He's not going to get away with that. Ten degrees to port,' he called out on the intercom to the control room below.

The helmsman swung the wheel and followed up with four blasts on the siren.

The captain stiffened, quivering from head to toe. He stared in disbelief at the siren and then at the helmsman. For a moment, he seemed lost for words. At last he recovered the power of speech and the words tumbled out in a torrent.

'You blithering idiot. How long have you lot been in this man's navy? Don't you know that four blasts mean SHIP OUT OF CONTROL?' He shook his head in disbelief. 'I'll never live it down,' he gasped and gazed around the harbour as if to look for an escape route. 'Lieutenant, take his name. And if it ever happens again,' he added, 'I'll have you all on a charge.'

For several more minutes he peered around the harbour to see if anyone had noticed the gaffe, which he obviously took as a personal affront. After a while (the tanker having passed close by in the meantime), he seemed to calm down a bit and he stopped pacing up and down on the bridge, peering through his telescope every now and again to make sure that nobody was setting out to rescue us. After a few moments more, he settled for a gruffly muttered, 'Huh, call yourselves seamen' and returned again to the business of getting the boat into port.

Half an hour later we were safely tied up at the dockside and the incident was forgotten in the hurly-burly of arrival at a new port and all the tasks which had to be completed before we could relax a bit and have some shore leave. It was only then that we were able to make our way into the actual town of Valletta, since the *Sturdy* had tied up at a berth in the port and was some distance even from the main dock gates. First we had to pick our way past both the local Dghaisa boats that serviced the ships anchored out in the harbour and the 'Goffa' boys milling on the quayside looking for business.

Once we had finally extricated ourselves from persistent entreaties to buy their souvenirs (or occasionally, their sisters), we spotted the Dreadnought pub at the dock gates. To both our surprise and pleasure, we saw that it sold English beers. The Dreadnought had been a magnet for British sailors long before we got there, but we reasoned that if it had been good enough for them, then it probably would be for us as well. We headed off in its direction.

While Bernie ordered the first round, I wandered over to the gallery of photographs hanging up on the walls. I found myself faced by pictures of the hundreds of naval ships that had called in to Grand Harbour over the years. It was almost a history of the modern navy itself. As we downed the first beers that we had drunk for at least a couple of weeks I realised that we were part of a long naval drinking tradition.

Several beers later, we decided to head off once more towards the town proper. We gave the long climb up the Custom House steps a miss and opted instead for the rickety, wire mesh-sided lift that limped up and down the front of the cliff face. Then, when we had reached the top, we wandered off to mingle with the locals on Republic Street, which seemed to be one of the main shopping streets. There we discovered several shops that sold, amongst other things, the Maltese lace that was one of the most popular gifts to take back home.

By the time we had tired of shopping, darkness had begun to set in and we decided it was time to eat instead. Since there were six of us it took a little time to sort out, but we finally agreed on one of the establishments that had a board advertising fish and chips outside. Although they probably weren't exactly a local delicacy, it did seem safer than experimenting with the local food. At least we would be able to tell whether it was any good or not – and it was. Not quite the same soggy chips or thick batter that we were used to back home, and they didn't have any mushy peas either, but it was still a good effort! By the time we set out to sample the nightlife an hour or two later, we were all feeling in good spirits. Naturally, we headed for the infamous 'Gut' area.

Crossing over Republic Street again, we headed off into a narrow street aptly known as the 'Gut', though according to Charlie, who knew because he had been to Valletta before, it was actually called Strada Streta or Strait Street. It ran all the way to Floriana at the other end of Grand Harbour – assuming you ever reached that far.

At the Valletta end the Gut was no more than 10ft wide. It was lined with bars, restaurants, noisy dives that were euphemistically called music halls, gambling casinos, live pornography shows, and hundreds of other thinly disguised brothels. At this time of the night most of the girls seemed to be outside, lining the narrow street and trying to entice customers with calls of 'inside boys, big eats'. When Steve assured one of them that he had already had his dinner, he wasn't really surprised to get the invitation to 'f*** off'.

None of us were really in the mood to try out their promises of a good time, largely through a fear of catching a 'dose'. Another reason was that few of the girls really warranted a second look and in my case it was through lack of money as well. Not only had I had inherited the sailor's sense of pride in not 'having to pay for it', as a lowly part-timer I couldn't afford anything else.

If I'd joined the services with any ideas about the navy subsidising my lascivious desires, they had quickly been dispelled. It didn't take long to find out that national servicemen weren't paid very much, and was one of the reasons I had volunteered for service in submarines where they got a bit of extra remuneration. I also found out that for the final six months of my national service I would be paid the same as the regulars and I could afford to 'splash out' a bit.

In the meantime I had to watch the pennies. Most of the time at sea there wasn't much to spend it on – except of course gambling, which was frowned upon by the authorities. Servicemen tended to save it up for the next 'run ashore' and then splurge it all in one go. I was no exception and most of what little money I had tended to go on alcohol. We concentrated on getting as much spirits inside ourselves as possible.

We started at 'Dirty Dick's' bar, where I could just about afford to try one of their layered, multi-coloured, rainbow cocktails. From then on I used what remaining small change was left to concentrate on the much cheaper local beer, and although I was making the drinks last, I began to notice that they were starting to take effect. It didn't need much persuasion to move on to the promised delights of the Silver Dollar dance hall and its blaring, jukebox music.

Conversation was interrupted for a while and we jigged around with a few of the girls. Eventually, after a few more rounds, we decided that it was time to move on again and we went round the corner to another bar, the Egyptian Queen. By that time, I was beginning to see things in a bit of a blur and would have been happy to lie down somewhere and go to sleep.

Charlie Summers, who seemed to have an unhealthy knowledge of the Gut, declared that we had to visit the New Life to see if the Sparrow was there. Translated, I discovered that this meant we had to go a little further along the narrow alleyway to another bar which, to give it its full name, was called the New Life Music Hall. There we might catch a glimpse of one the Gut's better-known female characters, who went by the nickname of the 'Sparrow'. I think someone said her real name was Maria or something like that, but by that time I wasn't taking a lot of notice.

I had perked up quite a lot by the time we finally reached the crowded bar of the New Life. It appeared that the Sparrow was in residence and had started going through her most popular act. Egged on by the cheering crowd, she was already halfway through her routine. It apparently involved sitting, largely unclothed, on the top of the bar near one end, with her legs spread wide apart. Meanwhile enthusiastic customers rolled coins along the surface of the bar from the opposite end. She kept any money that she could 'catch'! High denomination silver coins seemed to be her favourites, though probably they came in a variety of different currencies from several parts of the world.

By the time we had managed to push our way to the end of the bar furthest away from her (and with the best view) she had amassed a good deal of change. I just had time to notice the sign hanging above the bar reading 'clients are requested not to leave their stools whilst the bar is in motion' when I saw Steve trying to attract our attention.

'Hey, gather round,' I heard him call, his words only just carrying above the cheering of the spectators. 'I've got an idea.'

As we crowded round him, I saw that he had taken a cigarette lighter out of his pocket and was using the lighted flame to heat up a half-a-crown piece that he held tentatively by the edges. Then, when it had got so hot that he could hardly hold it any more, we dutifully cleared a path so that he could get to the bar and he sent the coin on its way, rolling along the bar top towards its target.

For the next five minutes or so, the bar was a centre of intense activity. First there were screams and a lot of swearing coming from the direction of the Sparrow. This was quickly followed by the sound of shouting and scuffling, fists flying and things being thrown about. There was a general stampede towards the entrance and I felt myself being pushed and punched. I was doing my best to retaliate, whilst at the same time trying to follow the others when, as if by magic, a couple of naval patrolmen and a very large Maltese policeman appeared in the doorway of the small bar.

I heard later that the latter represented the local law around the Gut, such as it was! He went by the nickname of 'Tiny', apparently because nobody had got on intimate enough terms with him to discover his real name. At the newcomer's appearance, the bar seemed to clear dramatically and we were legging it with everyone else back towards the town centre. From there we went stumbling down the long, steep Admiralty Steps towards the dockyard. Or, at least, most of us stumbled down the steps, but in Charlie's case, he rolled down some of them. Luckily, he escaped with just a few bruises. Then, with Steve and I on either side supporting him, we eventually got back to where our boat was berthed. Unfortunately, just as we were about to stumble back on board, Charlie discovered that somewhere on the way he had lost the lace handkerchiefs bought for his wife. He must have dropped them when he had taken a fall on the steps.

It took all our efforts to stop him from going back to look for them and then to quieten him down enough for us to tentatively approach the floodlit gangway. Luckily, the officer on watch had probably experienced some pretty unusual events in his time, and the sight of us trying to walk in a straight line up on to the deck, give a faltering salute and finally make our way down to our bunks didn't even cause him to raise an eyebrow.

Chapter 15

SICILIAN DROP-OUT

A few days later, having taken on board another load of fuel and supplies and having replaced Charlie's lost lace handkerchiefs, we slipped our berth, negotiated our way out of the harbour, and headed north for Sicily. The rest of the fleet having gone its own separate ways, we spent some time properly testing out the *Sturdy*'s refit – as well as our own makeshift repairs. We dived a couple of times, then ran at snorkel depth for a while, until we'd all had about enough and eventually surfaced and proceeded on the diesel engines alone. The seas were choppy, and there was a threat of rain. The skipper often took to carrying a rolled umbrella under his arm on the bridge rather than the more usual telescope. 'In case of showers,' he told anyone who was foolish enough to ask. Since he was wearing slippers at the time, it all seemed a little odd to everyone else around him.

Then one morning, while we were still out of sight of any land, the radar operator reported that he had detected an unknown ship rapidly approaching. The skipper, who was up on the bridge at the time, immediately raised his telescope and smartly put it to his eye. Except, of course, it wasn't his telescope at all, but the rolled umbrella he was carrying, the end of which unfortunately then caused him a painful stab in the eye. He swore in pain, but luckily there was no permanent damage. He went around with an improvised patch over the eye for several days and insisted on bathing it with a concoction of boiled seaweed, prepared for him by the cook.

Later that day, a notice appeared in the mess room pointing out that umbrellas weren't part of the standard naval uniform and they weren't to be used by anyone, under threat of immediate punishment. Naturally, the next day umbrellas suddenly appeared everywhere; sticking out of gun barrels, tied to the flag mast, inside cupboards – all over the boat in fact. Where they all came from, I've no idea!

Naturally enough, the captain was livid. He promised to have the first lieutenant put on a charge unless he found out who was responsible. And in addition he wouldn't speak to the rest of the officers for several days, but thankfully a couple of incidents on the way helped take his mind off the umbrella episode and all had been forgotten by the time we reached our next destination. First we stopped off to give assistance to a broken-down trawler and soon afterwards we stalked a Russian ship to see where it was going.

The trawler was an Italian ship. We had picked up its distress call on the radio at about breakfast time and finding that we weren't far away, we changed course to offer assistance. It turned out that the fuel pump had packed up. A couple of our mechanics went on board by dinghy and between them they soon sorted it out. By lunchtime, we had got them under power again and they were making their way back to port. By way of return we had the very welcome gift of freshly caught fish. By this time, our chef's culinary skills had been mostly reduced to wielding a tin-opener so everyone considered it a pretty fair trade.

It was later the next day that our lookout sighted the Russian ship away in the distance on our port side. We had picked something up on the radar screen a bit earlier, but we had gone in closer to investigate. The radar blip turned out to be one of the early Russian Type 56 cruisers. The skipper reckoned it was returning to its Black Sea base at Sevastopol or somewhere like that. Just out of interest and to see if they would spot us, we shadowed it for a while at snorkel depth. We'd really only used the snorkel (or snort as it tended to be nicknamed) for short periods, following the refit in Portsmouth, since the only opportunities had been during the refit trials and for the NATO exercises. This was the first time we would have a chance of using it for any length of time and finding out if we could avoid detection.

The snorkel tube on a submarine was somewhat similar to that sometimes used by a swimmer. With it, he can breathe with his head underwater near the surface and at the same time observe what was going on below. Only in the submarine's case it was to let the diesel engines 'breathe' whilst we were submerged but at the same time allowing us to see what was going on overhead!

When a submarine is travelling on the surface in its normal running position, the snorkel tube is locked either in its parked position on top of the deck or, in some designs, retracted like a periscope. Only when the boat starts to submerge is the operating handle in the control room moved to its dive state and the tube automatically raised into the upright position. The submarine can then run on its diesel engines while at periscope depth of about 6ft below the sea's surface – albeit at a reduced speed. In our case, this was usually not much more than 5 or 10 knots.

Usually, only the tops of the periscope and the snorkel tube project above the water's surface, making the submarine extremely difficult to see from another ship, particularly in a choppy sea. The thing you have to be careful about is that the engine exhaust doesn't give you away, by making a lot of smoke and noise. Assuming that an enemy doesn't spot you using sophisticated ASDIC equipment, the boat can then proceed happily on its engines just below the surface. Alternatively, it can recharge the batteries and be ready to dive completely.

Unlike a swimmer's snorkel tube, the submarine doesn't rely on a ping-pong ball or some similar device to prevent seawater getting into the tube, which could occur every time waves break over the top of the tube or the end inadvertently dips beneath the surface. It's not easy to keep a submarine trimmed at the right depth all the time, particularly in rough weather. Waves come at you from all directions – and at varying heights as well!

To stop it filling up with water, a submarine's snorkel tube is fitted with fail-safe sensors, both to detect when waves are breaking over the top or if it dips below the surface. When either of these things occurs, a head-valve automatically closes and the engines temporarily draw their induction air from within the boat. Unfortunately this doesn't do much for the efficiency of the engines, since the exhaust can become noisy (hence the term 'snort') as well as smoky – and it's not much fun for the crew either!

Luckily, the designers had also thought of this, so vacuum sensors detect if the pressure of air within the hull is becoming too low for safety. In this case the diesel engines automatically shut down and prevent any further air being drawn out of the boat. If needs be, the crew can also use the oxygen replenishment system. Everyone can then literally breathe a sigh of relief! We shadowed the Russian ship for a while, but boringly it kept radio silence and took no notice of us at all. Either it hadn't detected our presence or, more likely, it couldn't be bothered.

We shadowed it for a few hours and then the Jimmy decided he'd had enough. He changed course for Sicily.

Soon afterwards, we came back up to the surface and stowed the snorkel. We made better speed on the top. The boat was not quite as steady, particularly as the sea was a bit choppy, but we could leave a hatch open in the conning tower and the air down below in the mess felt a lot fresher. There was also fresh fish for supper. Things could have been a lot worse!

The *Sturdy* followed the coast around to the north-west of the island and passed through the breakwater into the harbour at Palermo. Then, after a bit of to-ing and fro-ing, we eventually drew up at the old Arab section of the port, known as Kalsa.

During the war, Palermo had been an important base for German and Italian fleets and as a result it had been practically levelled by the Allies in one night of heavy bombing. Few of the original buildings now remained, except for a few scruffy drinking houses which still bore the hammer and sickle of the local communist party who appeared to be running the place. There they dispensed a poisonous brew, both to the locals who were seemingly immune and to Jolly Jack Tar who knew no better. After a while we discovered that it was largely because there was no other alternative.

Next to the quay was a well-stocked souvenir shop, run by a middle-aged couple – she thin and wiry, with quick, darting, restless eyes and he, short, fat, smelling of homemade wine and of a rather excitable disposition. The town, or what was left of it, was still rife with vendettas. Any sailor taking more than a casual interest in any Sicilian wives or daughters risked a thorough beating – or worse! The wives on the other hand saw our arrival as a welcome relief from the frustrations and disputes they had with their husbands, both in and out of bed. In the end it didn't seem to make any difference, considering the regularity with which they were expected to bear children.

There was still an anti-British sentiment amongst a lot of the locals, together with a suspicion of all foreigners in general; a leftover from the recent world war and the communist control, I guessed.

We didn't have to wait long for a sample of their welcome. As we were sitting down to dinner on the first night there, the sky started to rain down with rocks and stones uprooted from the pitted cobblestone quayside and the nearby bombed-out buildings. The hail of stones continued for some time, while the quartermaster took refuge behind the periscope housing on the bridge. Finally it subsided as the attackers tired of their assault, and a couple of local policeman who had been standing chatting nearby soon drifted away, having looked on with little or no interest.

Next day, despite the far-from-welcoming reception, the quay's small souvenir shop was full with the ship's crew. They crowded around the souvenir-laden tables where the trinkets and gifts were on display for all to handle and inspect. Meanwhile, the proprietor and his wife tried unsuccessfully to both serve the milling crowds and also to keep an eye on the laden tables nearby. The husband obviously suspected that as fast as one matelot had paid for an item at the counter, others were stuffing unpaid-for goods down their shirtfronts from the nearby tables. He could have been right for all I knew. The excitable Sicilian owner got ever redder in the face, breathing fiery alcoholic fumes over the clientele and getting more and more worked up in his efforts to protect his wares. At last, with a bellow of anger, and waving his arms in the air, he let out a stream of what I assumed were Italian obscenities. Then, producing a massive revolver from a drawer at the back of the shop, he brandished it threateningly in the faces of those nearest to him.

'Thieves, banditos,' he roared, as everyone scattered. 'I shoota you all.'

It didn't do much for his business and after that we tended to give his souvenir shop a wide berth – and I never did find out if the revolver was loaded!

We stuck it out for a couple more days and then, since the town offered so little in the way of entertainment, the skipper decided one afternoon to send a small group of us off on a banyan party. It was probably intended as a way of avoiding any possible problems with the local residents.

Six of us set off along the coastline in a hired dinghy, passing by a number of small inlets and bays until after a while we had left the town well behind. Eventually, having tired of drifting slowly with the breeze, the chief, who was in charge, decided to pitch our tents on a flat strip of land that we could see in a cove up ahead. At one end there was also a shallow beach where we could land the boat safely.

After offloading the supplies and equipment, and having made sure the boat was securely tied up, we found a suitable spot inland well away from the beach and pitched the tents. A couple of hours later, with the sleeping bags prepared for the night and having cooked and eaten a lavish meal on a fire made from the plentiful stocks of driftwood around the beach, most of the party lay back for a well-earned rest. It should have been a welcome change from the cramped quarters on board the *Sturdy*, but by the time darkness had begun to fall, boredom had set in. Against my better judgement, I let myself be persuaded to join a couple of the others in 'having a look around'. So, carrying a few of the bottles of beer we had brought with us, we set off to explore.

At the far side of the grassy area we could just make out a narrow, rough path which we tried to follow by the light of our torches. Then twenty minutes later, after walking through a small area of woods in the semi-darkness, we reached the far side and the trees began to thin out and in the distance we could make out the lights of what looked like a large estate. Where there's an estate, we thought, there must be a vineyard. So, pausing only to finish off the bottles of beer, we pushed on in the dark, but as we neared the buildings, the dim light from the torches showed a low line of bushes and trees in front of us.

They appeared to form a hedge all around the main property, so following it around we found a small gap and tried to push our way through. The snapping and crashing that followed sounded extremely loud in the quiet of the night and sure enough, before we had even managed to finish pushing our way through the gap, a dog started to bark loudly from the direction of the house. It wasn't long before a chorus of other dogs had joined in from somewhere nearby.

In something approaching panic we turned and pushed our way back through the hedge before hastily returning the way we had come. It wasn't until we had got as far as the welcoming shelter of the woods that I ventured a glance back to see if we were being followed. At that moment, there was a bright flash and loud explosion from the direction of the house and what must have been lead pellets splattered through the tops of the trees above us. I hadn't time to reflect on the apparently plentiful supply of guns in the area before we decided it would be prudent to continue our hasty retreat.

It was still comparatively early in the evening and after some discussion (and having established that no one was following behind) we took to another path off at right angles and gave the house as wide a berth as possible. The path seemed to lead out of the woods and across some open, rough ground before setting off inland. A quarter of an hour later and now quite a long way from the camp, we could see lights ahead – probably a village or small town, we guessed. It was proving to be warm and thirsty work making our way by flickering torchlight over the uneven ground and we were beginning to be sorry that we had finished off all the beer. It was in the vain hope that we might be able to buy a fresh supply that we set off in the direction of the lights.

Soon we caught up with three figures going more or less in the same direction, one of whom was carrying an oil lantern. As we came nearer, they caught sight of us and stopped as we approached the group cautiously. At least, if there was going to be trouble, there were as many of us as there were of them! Judging by the look of their clothes, they were probably farmers or farm workers of some sort. Since we were also dressed in working clothes (or what the navy liked to call the 'No.8s'), we seemed to fit in all right. Even so we were both relieved and a bit surprised to gather from their greetings that even after they had realised we were from the submarine tied up in their town they still appeared to be friendly. We hadn't forgotten the reception that we received when we arrived in Palermo, but apparently they came from a completely different era to the young attackers.

In faltering Italian, and with a lot of signs and arm waving, we tried to explain that we were looking for somewhere to get a drink. This seemed to strike the right chord with them and it produced a lot more signs, arm waving and back slapping. Eventually we gathered that if we liked to follow them we would be able get a drink just a bit further down the street.

Unfortunately, it seemed that the little Italian we were able to summon up between us was proving to be of small use. They either had strong accents or they used a Sicilian dialect that we couldn't follow. Luckily it didn't seem to matter. We were managing to have some sort of exchange with them and they showed every sign of being friendly towards us. With a little trepidation we fell into step alongside and waited to see where it would lead us.

After a few minutes we found that we were approaching a main road, with some occasional passing traffic in the form of a truck or a bicycle. We turned a corner and there, at the edge of a small wood and partly concealed from the road by a wall, we came across an old, derelict, Second World War concrete and brick pillbox. An equally old and rusting bicycle was leaning against it. The saddle was falling to pieces and several of the spokes were obviously missing. Through the slits of the pillbox where the guns would have been in earlier times, clouds of smoke drifted upwards in to the night sky.

To our surprise, our new companions led the way down some concrete steps, round a corner and through a narrow entrance. We discovered that the smoke was coming from a small fire in one corner of the room and by its light we could make out a hunched-up figure that lay on a rickety bed alongside one of the walls. He was obviously asleep and snoring loudly.

Although the room was a bit muggy, it was quite warm and cosy inside the pillbox. A few stools and upturned wooden boxes were placed in front of the fire and five medium-sized wooden barrels stood in the corner. There was a rough, wooden cupboard by the bedside. Going over to the figure on the bed, one of the Sicilians gave it a sharp prod in the ribs and, after a few moments of grunting and following some shaking, the figure finally lurched to his feet.

He turned out to be a farming companion of our newly found friends and after one of the others had obviously explained our presence, he launched into a flowery speech of welcome – not a word of which we understood. Still, he was obviously a pal of the others, so we took it as a good sign. He motioned for us to take a seat on the stools and boxes as he opened the cupboard and took out an assortment of mugs and glasses. All were of different size and shape, but all had a well-used look about them. Then, going over to the barrels in the corner, he turned a tap and filled them to the brim, the firelight showing a dark red stream of obviously homebrewed wine. The assorted drinks were passed around and after a number of toasts we took a deep gulp from the generously filled containers.

Most sailors aren't what you'd call strangers to alcohol; the daily ration of rum helps to see to that. Many are pretty hardened drinkers, and by that time I was no exception. I had served enough time in submarines and drunk enough 'pussers' rum to have become fairly well acclimatised. I probably even had a permanent level of alcohol in my body. So although the wine was rougher and stronger than the average plonk we were used to, we were soon refilling our glasses from the barrel and noisily joining in the conversation. At first we didn't really understand what they were talking about and I doubt if they understood us either. But it turned out that a couple of them had fought for the partisans at the end of the war and had learnt a few words of English from their contact with the Allies. By a series of extremely rude signs, they also indicated what they thought of the communists.

Their smattering of a common language helped the flow of conversation considerably and it also explained why we had been welcomed as friends. Before long we were talking, gesticulating and swearing as loudly as they were and doing our best to join in the discussions. These seemed to cover the universal topics of women, politics and football. Not necessarily in that order of course and often all at the same time, which didn't help much, but by that time nobody seemed to notice.

It turned out that our host's name was Giovanni. He lived on a farm about five miles away, together with his wife, mother, father, grandfather, mother-in-law and innumerable children, all of whom seemed to be dependent on him for support. According to the way Giovanni told it, at the same time as being reliant on him, they all gave him a hard time. Whereas what he really wanted was a quiet life. So, by the time winter was nearly over and the sowing was finished, he usually couldn't stand their arguing any more and he would get out his old bicycle one night, ride over to the pillbox and live there in peace on his own for a month or two, with only occasional visits from his friends for company. This would last until the summer, or he had started to miss his wife or the wine ran out – whichever came first. Sometimes affairs of the farm needed his attention, or the harvest needed gathering. Then he would ride back home again on his rickety transport, only to find that in the meantime his wife had presented him with another child!

When he returned home, there usually followed a short altercation with his wife and then there would be a grand reconciliation and period of making up. The following spring, after the sowing had been attended to and his animals having successfully produced their offspring, he would collect his fishing rod and pedal off once more to his pillbox retreat.

'I reck'n ee's got it made,' sighed Smithy, his eyes taking in the bed and the barrels of wine, his speech by now starting to get slurred. 'Himagine lying here with all them barrels only a couple of feet away. And all the while, when he gets the urge, his wife's only five miles cycle away. It cert'nly beats bein' in the navy!'

By now the proceedings were beginning to slow down. Giovanni reached under his bed and pulled out a bottle of amber liquid, pouring a generous helping into everyone's glasses and mugs before making a toast to our good health and then downing his own drink in a single gulp. His companions followed suit; so not to be outdone and not wishing to give offence, we did the same. Too late, I realised that I had made a big mistake! I've no idea what the liquid was, or even if it was intended for drinking, but immediately it reached my stomach the concoction appeared to produce a small explosion inside and decided that it ought to come back up again. As I brought it all up and made a stumbling dash for the doorway, I noticed vaguely that most of it had gone in the fire. It had immediately burst into flames and threw burning logs out of the grate.

Sometime later I had recovered sufficiently to go back inside. There I was greeted with shouts of mirth at my expense.

'I believe Giovanni uses it for lighting the fire,' explained Whitey, seriously.

Soon afterwards Giovanni lay down on his bed and went off to sleep again. We decided it was probably time to leave, and with the snores of Giovanni filling the smoke-ridden room, we trooped out into the night leaving him to continue his interrupted snooze.

Together with our newly found drinking friends who were going in the same direction, we made our way back to the spot where we had first met. There we said goodbye and, after a series of handshakes, embraces and back-slapping, we concentrated all our efforts on trying to follow the path back through the woods and on to our beds; this time without either being shot at or disturbing the local four-legged community. The only one who didn't seem pleased at our return was the chief. He was officially in charge of the group and it was his sleep that we had managed to disturb.

Next morning we broke camp, stowed everything in the dinghy and made our way slowly back to where the *Sturdy* was berthed. While we'd been away, we found that there had been more spasmodic stone throwing. Also a hastily formed ship's team had lost at football to the local side, the chef had cut his thumb opening a tin of beans, and there'd been another incident at the souvenir shop on the quay. One way and another, it had been quite an eventful visit but I doubt if there were many tears shed by either visitors or residents when we left Palermo next day and headed for home.

After a stop off at Gib' to take on fuel and supplies, we spent a few more days carrying out a series of exercises with the home fleet. It was another fortnight or so before we eventually passed the Isle of Wight once more and made our way back into the bustle of Portsmouth harbour. Then, having successfully negotiated our passage through a clutch of ferries making their way seaward, we drew alongside the massive stonework of Fort Blockhouse, closed off both of the submarine's engines, and finally tied up.

Chapter 16

Victory in Sight

By the time I got back to HMS *Dolphin*, I had realised that my two years of national service was practically finished. The last two years had passed by quicker than I realised. It seemed like only yesterday that as a raw recruit I had gone to HMS *Raleigh* for basic training. But here I was just two years later, hopefully a bit older and wiser, being thrown out into the wide world again. Or so I thought. Perhaps I had no more idea of what I wanted to do in life than when I came into the forces, but at least it didn't concern me quite as much. I felt more confident that, whatever was in store for me, I had as good a chance of success as the next man – well, almost! I collected my kit bag, hammock and civvy street clothes and managed to get a lift in a navy truck to the demob centre at Victory Barracks.

When I arrived, all the old faces were already there. I hadn't seen most of them since our training days at HMS *Raleigh*. As far as I knew I was the only one from our original group to have ended up in the submarines branch and so I hadn't seen anything of the others for over a year. There was a lot of catching up to do.

We unpacked for the last time in the passing out mess to which we were directed and the place took on the atmosphere of an old school reunion. It wasn't that we had been anything like lifelong friends. We were just a group of strangers who had gone through a shared experience together. Stewart Robins probably summed it up best when he remarked, half-jokingly, that 'some blokes probably remember their mates better than their first girlfriend'. It was an opportunity to catch up with everyone else's experiences over the last couple of years and also to make plans for the future when we 'got out'. The duties that we were given at *Victory* weren't all that onerous, so the time passed convivially and quickly.

I discovered that Jock McLeod, whose career with Motherwell Football Club had been interrupted by his unwelcome period of service, had actually spent very little time at all in what could be called the forces. After his basic training the navy had been keen to employ his talents on the football field instead, and he spent most of the two years playing for the navy against army and RAF teams. What little spare time that it left him he spent at his home either resting or training with his old team. It had already been agreed with the club that after completing his service he would be taking up his career again where he had left off. As far as he was concerned, it had been a wasted two years.

Tim Reynolds was another of our intake who would have preferred not to have endured his national service. Not only had he been married just before he was called-up, but he had also taken over the running of his father's farm in Hampshire. Apart from missing his new family, he had been more than a bit upset to find that he wasn't going to see his first lot of seed crops growing and harvesting either. Consequently he couldn't wait for the two years to finish. He had hardly even seen his recently born son. The fact that he had managed to get transferred to a job in a Pompey barracks and he had been able to get home some weekends had made him even more frustrated.

Seemingly Wally Hargraves had been another accident of the system – literally! He had slipped and fallen down the boiler room ladder of the first ship that he had stepped aboard. After a period spent convalescing he was invalided out of the navy and in the end he only served a total of about ten months of his service.

But not everyone was fed up with their time in the services. At least two of our group, Phil Edwards and Ron Williams, had made up their minds to sign on again as regulars when they finished their time. They reckoned that the navy gave them a career and better wages and future than the ones they could look forward to on the 'outside'. Since they didn't have any family dependents and they hadn't trained in any craft nor had any qualifications either, you could see their point. For the rest of us, we would take away a mixture of some new skills or experiences, some lasting friendships and a lot of memories. In a few cases, some of the more hardened criminals would also take away a collection of the Admiralty's property.

From my own perspective, I could point to the fact that I had learned to tie some useful knots, I had become proficient in various new swear words, had made a propeller casting while at sea and could even darn my own socks. I could 'sling' a hammock, escape from a flooded submarine and at a pinch could even remember which side of a boat was port and which starboard. In addition I had unselfishly and generously donated my meagre wages to the alcoholic drinks industries of various countries. That seemed to me to be quite enough to be going on with!

It was whilst we were reminiscing and making plans for the future over a drink in the local pub that Taffy came up with the idea of leaving the navy with something to remember us by. The thought seemed to catch on, and several increasingly hazardous suggestions were put forward, before being regretfully dismissed as being either impractical or downright illegal. They included a number of proposals involving the admiral's car or inflated 'johnnies', before we finally decided that flying a skull and crossbones flag from the masts of HMS *Victory* would suit the bill nicely. We all agreed that it would have the required effect of embarrassing the Admiralty without actually causing any criminal damage.

The historic *Victory* was on show to the public in No.2 dry dock, only a few hundred yards behind our barracks. At nearly 230ft long and with its four huge masts rising over 200ft into the air above sea level, the massive wooden warship was an imposing sight – at least in the daylight! We were actually planning to visit it at night which was probably a different matter altogether. We didn't have much time in which to plan, since we were all due to be discharged in three days' time; so, next lunchtime a three-man team went over to take a look at the site and make a note of any likely difficulties.

As the only surviving ship from the American War of Independence, the French and the Napoleonic Wars, HMS *Victory* was a popular attraction to tourists and locals alike. Knowing that at one time it was commanded by no less a heroic figure than Admiral Nelson only added to the interest. Everyone wanted to see the spot on the quarterdeck where he had been tragically struck down by French musket fire as he was giving orders to his crew. Most of the ship was open to the public, although at the time they were still doing some restoration and building work. That meant that there were plenty of workmen likely to be in the area and also that there would be some lighting even late into the evenings. So far, so good!

The ship was located in the middle of the nearby dock, where it was held upright by a number of wooden supports underneath the ship and a series of wooden fenders propped against its sides. The fenders were to keep it away from the edge of the dock. A gangplank allowed visitors access to the gun deck and this appeared to be a permanent fixture. By the look of it, even if the gangplank was closed when we tried to gain access there were still plenty of other ways in. Most of the gun ports were left open and even though cannon barrels were sticking out of most of them it looked to us as if there was still enough space to squeeze past them and get inside the ship. There should be plenty of gun ports from which to choose.

The *Victory* carried over a hundred large cannons on board, as well as the two short, stubby, devastating 68-pounders, known as carronads. These could be directed downwards from the upper deck and used to rake nearby enemy ships with a frightening blanket of grapeshot. It must have all but eliminated any opposition. The *Victory*'s vast anchor was hanging against the side of the ship and supported by a wooden cradle. Its thick, supporting rope hung down in a long loop near to the edge of the dock.

Access to the main deck shouldn't have been a problem. From there, we could swing out over the bulwarks and climb the thin 'ratlines' which in times past had been used as a ladder to hoist the sails. From the ratlines we would be able to reach the 'fighting top'. This was the lookout platform the sailors could stand on, built around the mast high above the main deck. There were 'lubber holes' cut in the platform through which you could gain access to the horizontal 'yards' that jutted out just above. That was where the vast sails had originally been attached.

We decided that the first platform was as high as we would probably go – particularly in the dark – and we would attach the skull and crossbones flag by its corners somewhere nearby. From there it would be clearly visible from some distance away.

But finding a large skull and crossbones flag at such short notice proved to be a whole new problem. Try what may, we couldn't locate one anywhere. In fact, we had almost given up all hope of finding one when Whitey remembered that he'd seen one hanging on display at the Naval Museum just outside the dockyard entrance. He'd been there recently with his parents when they had come down from London to meet him. It was our last hope and so by popular demand he was hastily despatched to 'borrow' it!

It was early evening before he returned, triumphantly bearing his prize. The delay was due to him having to wait until just before closing time before the room was clear of people. Only then could he remove the flag without being noticed.

There was little time to lose, since we would soon be leaving the barracks for good. The only part of our service that remained was for us to have a medical inspection and then pay a visit to the dentist. Finally, in two days time, on the day that we would be leaving, there was to be a passing-out parade to which parents and relatives were invited. If we were going to leave something to be remembered by, then it would have to be tonight. All of us would be dispersing soon afterwards and going our separate ways. There wouldn't be another chance.

Only four of us were to actually be involved in fixing up the flag. That way there was less likelihood of being spotted and fewer people to be in trouble if they were. Somehow, I got included in the four volunteers. Maybe I was more foolhardy than some of the others, but at least we decided to wait until about nine o'clock that night, to let things settle down a bit before we set off.

By the time we decided it was safe to leave, it had been dark for a while and there was a slight drizzle in the air. The wind had got up a bit as well, so there weren't likely to be too many people about either. The conditions seemed ideal. It helped that, since we were no longer going to be the navy's responsibility in a couple of days time, there was very little discipline or control of our movements. Getting out of the barracks in civilian clothes was probably going to be the easiest part.

It turned out that actually getting on board *Victory* was not quite as simple as we had imagined and it nearly put an end to all our plans.

We had got out of the barracks easily enough. We left by the back gates, out into the damp and dark dockyard, without any trouble. By leaving through the rear entrance, we could go directly into the dockyard. We wouldn't have to go through the main dockyard entrance and past any sentries.

The street at the back of the barracks led between large office buildings or stores and was lit here and there by a few lamp posts. A few windows were still brightly illuminated and one of the office blocks had scaffolding around it where renovation work was in progress. In less than five minutes from quitting the warmth of the barracks, we had turned a corner and there ahead of us we could make out the vast bulk of the

Victory. We had only passed one other person on the way there and he hadn't given us a second glance.

In the semi-darkness, the ship looked even more imposing up close than it had from a distance. The sides rose high above us, with two rows of threatening cannons jutting out from the large, square ports. Their outside doors were raised into the open position and only the short black ends of the cannon muzzles could be seen in the half-light. Looking upwards, we could just make out the huge masts, spars and rigging outlined against the darkened sky. It was going to be a long climb. Then, as we got nearer, we saw to our dismay that the third and lowest row of cannon ports had their doors closed, making any entrance through them impossible. The sloping gangway that bridged the gap from the quayside across to the entrance in the ship's middle gun deck was still in place, but what we hadn't bargained for was that the door into the ship itself was closed and locked. I suppose it had been too much to hope for that it might be left open at night!

The light drizzle was still falling and there was a thin mist in the night air. The area seemed deserted as we searched without success along the ship's side for a way in. We had all but given up when Pete said thoughtfully, 'There was a ladder back there tied to some scaffolding where they were renovating a building. Perhaps we could get in with that.' It was then that we realised what he had noticed.

It was probably going to be impossible to gain an access through the gun ports since we had already seen that the bottom row of cannon ports nearest to where the visitors entered all had their outside shutters closed. The middle and top gun decks did have their shutters wide open but would be too small for us to squeeze past the cannons; even if we could have reached them. But from where we stood on the gangway, the quarterdeck was only about 10 or 12ft above our heads. We were glad to see that in the days when *Victory* was built, space was at a premium and deck heights were suited to much shorter sailors. With any luck and a long ladder we could probably reach to the lower rail. It was well worth a try.

The dockside was still deserted as we made our way quickly back down the alleyway to the building where we had noticed the scaffolding. Sure enough, the higher floors were being worked on by means of various ladders and it didn't take us long to remove the ropes which held the lowest one in place. Between us we carried it back to the ship and placed it on the gangway, with the top end resting against the ship's side timbers. It reached up to a few feet below the rail around the quarterdeck, and within minutes we had climbed up one at a time and clambered over onto the deck itself. There followed a brief discussion in lowered tones as to whether we should try and pull the ladder up behind us where it couldn't be seen, but in the end we decided against it.

As we crossed the deck out of view from below, we saw by the light of our torches the plaque commemorating where Admiral Nelson had received his fatal wound. I hoped that it wasn't going to be some sort of omen! Pete, who at over 6ft tall and weighing 14 stone wasn't really built for climbing and didn't much care for heights either, volunteered to stay down on deck and keep an eye out for any signs of authority. That left Whitey (whose flag it was), Ken and I to climb up the 'standing rigging', using the trellis-like ratlines on each side of the ship. They rose above the bulwarks and went all the way up to the large platform 100ft or so up each mast.

We had taken the precaution of wearing trainers and using gloves, but climbing up the rigging still wasn't easy. The higher we rose, the stronger the wind blew and we began to sway around in the breeze. Luckily, as there was sufficient light from the dockyard for us not to need the light of our torches, it left our both hands free for the task of climbing.

It felt like an age of climbing and swaying around in the semi-darkness high above the deck below before we reached the first yardarm. In order to save a bit of time, we had already attached strong tie-ropes to the corners of the flag Whitey was carrying. Earlier, it had been decided to tie the lower corners on to the yardarm, then climb a bit higher and tie the top corners to the lower side of the 'fighting top' above. Unfortunately, it proved a bit more difficult in the wind and rain than we had bargained for. In the end, we decided that it would be easier to climb up on to the platform first, where we could then steady ourselves. That way we would feel a bit more secure when we came to fasten the corners of the flag. So we climbed up to the two small openings in the fighting top, one on either side of the mast, and once through, lay exhausted on the wet surface. At that moment I had a lot of sympathy for those earlier breed of sailors who had to scramble up in all weathers to set the sails.

Eventually, having secured the top corners of our flag to the rigging ropes nearby, we descended a little and tied the lower ends around the yardarm below. Finally, wet and tired, but triumphant, we made our way gingerly back down to the main deck while the large skull and cross-bones flapped somewhere in the darkness and wind high above.

We heard from Pete that there hadn't been much activity on the quay-side whilst we had been busy aloft. One or two people had passed by, but they had their heads held downwards in the drizzling rain and hadn't noticed anything unusual going on aboard the *Victory*. I imagine that everyone in the dockyard was so used to its presence that they didn't give it a second glance.

After carrying the ladder back to its original site and tying it to the scaffolding, we all made our way still unnoticed back into the barracks. By now it was well past 'lights out' time, but since supervision was so relaxed near to our leaving, we were able to give the others a (slightly embellished) account of the night's exploits before eventually everyone turned in for the night.

Next morning I had to attend the passing out medical and dentist appointments, which meant that I didn't get to see the fruits of our labours myself. Instead I had to make do with a report from Pete who had managed to get round to the *Victory* before they had removed the offending flag. For some reason, the authorities apparently didn't appre-ciate the pride of the British Navy flying a pirates' flag from its yardarm.

By mid-morning a crowd had gathered on the quay alongside the *Victory* and as they discussed down below what should be done about it, the pirates' flag continued to flap in the breeze overhead. The dock-yard workers flatly denied any responsibility and refused to climb up the rigging to get it down. Eventually an unwilling sailor was ordered to remove it instead. Naturally, he had to endure the embarrassment of jeers and catcalls from below as he climbed high aloft. The Admiralty knew they would never find the culprits and so confined themselves to issuing muted threats about what would happen if naval personnel turned out to have been involved and if it ever reoccurred. It appeared that we had got off lightly.

Meanwhile we had other things with which to occupy ourselves. The navy doctors and dentists pushed and prodded us and finally declared us all fit to return into the civilian world. Some of us were probably fitter and had better teeth than when we had joined! The rest of the morning was spent deep in elbow grease and boot polish. Best uniforms were cleaned and ironed until the mess began to look more like a Chinese laundry. Boots were buffed until you could see your reflection in their shine. Concertina creases in bell-bottom trousers were as sharp as the proverbial knife.

Probably it would be somewhat of an exaggeration to claim that a smart group of national service recruits marched to the strains of the Royal Navy Band that afternoon. On the other hand, it was certainly true that we would have been unrecognisable as the same rabble which had arrived at HMS *Raleigh* two years before. There was almost a feeling of pride in everyone, which certainly hadn't been there before. As we marched stiffly and more or less in step, at the same time saluting the Commander of the Fleet and the cheering crowd of family and relatives, even CPO Burt, our hard-to-please instructor, would probably have taken some satisfaction that day. We had definitely been better than the *Come Dancing* formations he had compared us with!

The mood and conversation in the pub that final evening was quieter and more subdued than usual, particularly after the excitement of the last few days. It was only then that I began to realise that I must have spent a fair proportion of the last two years in one pub or another.

The next morning, I walked out of the Victory Barracks for the last time. I was no longer in uniform. I remember it was the last day of October 1957 and autumn had arrived. Everyone said that the sixties was going to be an era of pop music, hippies, peace for all and free love. Songs by the Beatles and the Rolling Stones would be played everywhere. Soon, Harold Macmillan would reckon that we'd never had it so good. So why wasn't I dancing with joy? Surely I couldn't be having any regrets? Perhaps I had begun to realise that my regular, ordered (in more ways than one) and somewhat cosseted national service life was over. I would soon have to start taking some decisions for myself. In a strange way, the service may have actually prepared me for that. I was a bit more sure and confident about things than I had been when I had started my national service. Perhaps it was just the sign of the times. Or perhaps, in spite of the fact that recent events would indicate otherwise, I had grown up a bit. Who knows?

I made my way to the train station and went in to buy a ticket for home.

'Yes sir, where would you like to go?' enquired the attendant at the ticket office. It was then that I truly realised I was no longer in the services. I would have to get used to being called 'Sir' all over again.

ABBREVIATIONS AND ACRONYMS

I sometimes wonder if the forces invented acronyms. They certainly use them extensively, and navy servicemen often use initials instead of lengthy ranks or titles. Therefore, where I felt it was appropriate I have also used them, but since they may not be familiar to everyone, I have given a brief explanation below:

ASDIC   Was probably derived during the Second World War from Anti-Submarine Detection Investigation Committee, although it seems likely that no such committee existed

Chief   Chief Petty Officer

Civvy   Civilian

CPO   Chief Petty Officer

CTC, DC, DM (gases)   Gases derived from organophosphorous acid anhydrates which attack the nervous system

Dogwatch   Period of duty between 1600 and 2000hrs (4p.m. to 8p.m.)

HMS   Her (or His) Majesty's Ship

Jimmy	Captain
MoD	Ministry of Defence
NAAFI	Navy, Army and Air Force Institutes. Formed in 1921 to run forces recreational establishments
Oggin	Sea. Said to be a mispronunciation of the word ocean
PO	Petty Officer
PoW	Prisoner of War
Pompey	Portsmouth
SETT	Submarine Escape Training Tank
SONAR	Sound Navigation and Ranging
Tiffies	Graduate of the Marine Engineering Artificer Qualifying Course. Rank first introduced in 1868 with the transition from sail to steam propulsion. Final recruits passed out in 2010
Wren	Member of the Women's Royal Navy
WRN	Women's Royal Navy

Also published by The History Press:

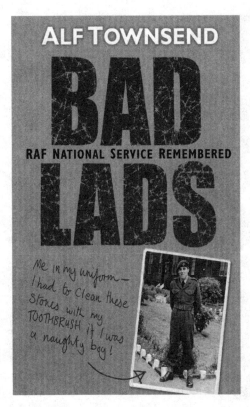

Bad Lads: RAF National Service Remembered

Alf Townsend

978-0-7524-6054-3

Between 1945 and 1963 over 2½ million eighteen-year-olds were called up for national service. Alf Townsend was one of them, and here he tells his story – the highs and lows of life as a lowly Aircraftman Second Class in the early 1950s. Before national service intervened Alf was 'heading down the criminal road at top speed', having grown up in a North London slum where money was short and local villains were revered.

Bad Lads is a warts and all account of Alf Townsend's time in the RAF, when he was transplanted into a completely new world of misfits and officer types, rogues and entertainers, all amusingly described in the author's inimitable style.

Submariners' News: The Peculiar Press of the Underwater Mariner

Keith Hall

978-0-7524-5793-2

For many years submariners produced 'local newspapers', reporting from the deep with a unique take on their unusual lifestyle. Held in much affection by submarine crews, they enjoyed a long period of popularity from the 1970s–1990s for their irreverent and decidedly un-PC approach to underwater living.

In this entertaining book, author Keith Hall examines the development of this strange branch of 'underwater journalism', collating the articles and anecdotes, jokes, cartoons and stories that have been published over the years to brighten up the lives of submariners far from home, providing an insight into the bizarre self-contained world of the submariner.